Kissing The Leper

Seeing Jesus in
the Least of These

Bible translations used:

The Holy Bible, New International Version®.© 1973, 1978, 1984 by International Bible Society. Used by permission of Zondervan Publishing House. All rights reserved.

King James Version, Public Domain.

The Message by Eugene H. Peterson, copyright © 1993, 1994, 1995, 1996, 2000, 2001, 2002. Used by permission of NavPress Publishing Group. All rights reserved.

New King James Version, Copyright © 1982 by Thomas Nelson, Inc. Used by permission. All rights reserved.

Italics herein were added by the author for emphasis, unless otherwise stated.

The testimonies herein are true, but I've indicated some name changes and incidental facts for the sake of confidentiality.

Cover design by Matt Borck (www.samuraimedia.net)
Cover photos by Sara Borck (www.saraborck.com)
Interior photos taken by members of Fresh Wind Christian Fellowship.
Printed in Canada by D.W. Friesen and Sons Ltd.

Library and Archives Canada Cataloguing in Publication

Jersak, Brad, 1964-
Kissing the leper : seeing Jesus in the least of these / Brad Jersak.
Includes bibliographical references.
ISBN 0-9780174-0-4
1. Minorities--Religious aspects--Christianity. I. Title.

BV4647.S9J47 2006 270.08 C2006-900573-7

To contact Brad or to get information on his seminars,
e-mail him at *info@freshwindpress.com.*

Fresh Wind Press
2170 Maywood Court
Abbotsford, BC Canada V2S 4Z1
www.freshwindpress.com

Kissing The Leper

Seeing Jesus in
the Least of These

Brad Jersak

freshwindpress

Dedication

To Rodney Jersak

My brother, my friend,
and founding director of
House of Hesed
HIV/AIDS transition house

"He defended the cause of the poor and needy,
and so all went well.
Is that not what it means to know me?"
declares the LORD.

Jeremiah 22:16

Contents

Contents

Christmas Beauty: 2005
Eugene H. Peterson

He had no form or comeliness
that we should look at him,
And no beauty that we should desire him.

Isaiah 53:2

A whiff. A beagle for beauty I sniffed
Monet's haystacks, van Gogh's sunflowers,
devoutly meditated Marilyn's breasts,
watched kingfishers—lost the scent.

> *Kiss the leper's wound: taste honey.*
> *Touch the blind eye: learn Braille.*
> *Keep vigil at the cradle: change diapers.*
> *Drink tears from the chalice: live eucharist.*

Happened on found things, found in gutters,
found on a cross, found under a stone,

> *heard in the whispering grass, heard in*
> *a tongue stammering sabacthani.*

Found when I wasn't looking, heard
when I wasn't listening. Found beauty.

Foreword

Jesus-Sightings

By Eugene Peterson

I AM A BIRDWATCHER. When another birdwatcher puts in a
book his or her observations and delight in bird-sightings in
forests and prairies and marshes, my observations are confirmed
and my delight deepens. I take special delight in sightings of
the shy and elusive, the Swainson's Thrush, the MacGillivray
Warbler.

I am also a Christian. When another Christian puts into a
book his or her observations and delight in Jesus-sightings on
streets and in sanctuaries and playgrounds, my observations
are confirmed and my delight deepens. I take special delight in
Jesus-sightings in crack houses and wheelchairs, refugee camps
and autistic children.

Brad Jersak's book is a gathering of field notes on Jesus-sightings among the disabled, the children, the prodigals, and the poor. He has a practiced and discerning eye and ear for bringing Jesus to notice among "the least of these" among whom Jesus is present to be fed and welcomed and clothed and cared for and visited. This is first-hand witness, a freshly articulated documentary, on Jesus' story of the sheep and goats (Matthew 25)—with an emphasis on the sheep who served Jesus when they didn't know they were serving him. The Jesus-sightings take place among the homeless and hungry, the addicts and prostitutes, the bisexual and rejected, the Down's Syndrome and misfits.

Our North American culture honors and celebrates the beautiful, the rich, and the accomplished with spotlighted, center-stage prominence and makes sure that the lepers and Lazarus are kept out of sight (and smell!) backstage. Too much of the church, to its immense shame, goes along with the culture.

But not Brad Jersak, a pastor of the congregation, "Fresh Wind Christian Fellowship," in Abbotsford, B.C. He makes common cause with St. Francis, who got his start in following Jesus by kissing a leper in Italy; with Mother Teresa who got her start caring for the homeless dying in the streets of Calcutta; and with Henri Nouwen who spent his last years as pastor to the severely disabled in Toronto's *L'arche Community.*

But Pastor Jersak doesn't just admire them and write about them. He *joins* them: he describes his congregation as a place where he sees and meets Christ within the structure of the "four pillars"—the disabled, the children, the prodigals, the poor—that comprise his congregation. His mostly local documentary is salted with further documentation from Africa, Burma and Haiti, Toronto, Edmonton and Winnipeg. These things were and are "not done in a corner" (Acts 26:26).

It turns out that Jesus' "sheep and goats" story continues to be documented in delightful ways but more often than not in the societal obscurity in which Jesus is, and always has been, most likely to be seen and heard, touched and fed.

Eugene H. Peterson
Professor Emeritus of Spiritual Theology
Regent College, Vancouver, B.C.
April 2006

As kingfishers catch fire, dragonflies dráw fláme
Gerard Manley Hopkins

As kingfishers catch fire, dragonflies dráw fláme;
As tumbled over rim in roundy wells
Stones ring; like each tucked string tells, each hung bell's
Bow swung finds tongue to fling out broad its name;
Each mortal thing does one thing and the same:
Deals out that being indoors each one dwells;
Selves—goes itself; myself it speaks and spells,
Crying Whát I do is me: for that I came.

Í say móre: the just man justices;
Kéeps gráce: thát keeps all his goings graces;
Acts in God's eye what in God's eye he is—
Chríst—for Christ plays in ten thousand places,
Lovely in limbs, and lovely in eyes not his
To the Father through the features of men's faces.

Introduction

The Blessing of Deeper Sight

By Andy MacPherson

A Saint is one who exaggerates what the world neglects.

G.K. Chesterton

A S CHILDREN OF GOD, WE ARE SAINTS. And yet
it is often those who press in deeper to the truths of God
that are considered "capital-S" Saints by the Church. They are
ones who have grasped the truth and then dared to live it. They
are men and women who fully believe God's promise to be close
to the lowly and oppressed, and so they stand courageously to
defend such people in the face of great opposition or indifference. Sometimes we exalt these people to mythical status in our
churches, but I fear that we also dehumanize them in the process,
pushing their contributions beyond our grasp into some godly

realm where we could never follow. So we claim their blessing on our lives, perhaps wearing their image on an amulet around our necks for good luck, and then live as though the path they walked is unattainable for us mere mortals.

I suspect that most saints would be aghast at such treatment, for no saint worthy of the name starts out desiring to be one. In fact, I would guess that in giving up their lives for God's sake, they have truly found themselves and would feel somewhat sheepish about being placed up on the pedestal of self-sacrifice. To see the great promises of God come alive in forgotten places and among forgotten people is the joy of the true saint. Such joy requires no reward greater than being allowed to continue to experience it. This joy is, in fact, open to all, for all can descend to poverty, but not all ascend to riches. A true and saintly path is one of hope for all of humanity, for it is a downward path we can all follow if we can get low enough and small enough to worm through the needle's eye of insignificance into the great courtyards filled with God's treasures.

I am told that I have a gift for loving people with mental and physical disabilities. Many times, people will tell me after a church service how much they enjoyed watching me move among them, hugging and blessing them. I appreciate such encouragement, but I find their praise somewhat embarrassing, since the blessing I receive back far outweighs what I give. I feel like a vampire who is encouraged for being so affectionate when in fact I have been sucking the lifeblood out of people.

> **To see the great promises of God
> come alive in forgotten places
> and among forgotten people is
> the joy of the true saint.**

Joan is a case in point. She is a mentally challenged friend who came to a Monday morning church service that we established for the disabled. She had just received her sight back through cataract surgery, and when I knelt down to welcome her, she reached out and cupped my face in her hands and just looked deeply at me. Talking is a challenge for her, yet as she mumbled away, staring into my eyes, I felt as though I was looking into the very eyes of Christ and hearing his muttered prayers. She was seeing me for the first time. As we gazed at one another, she didn't even blink, as though even a slight interruption of the sight of me was too costly. I was being *seen,* and I knew it. She saw nothing in me that made her want to turn away. When she eventually stopped staring at me with those brand new eyes, she put her arms around me and held me for a long time. I could feel the power of her affection as the power of God's affection for me. The amazing thing about this meeting was that it was my first meeting *ever* with Joan... and yet instantly the connection of care changed me. I looked at her in wonder and awe, because she looked at me with wonder and awe. I could not look at her as a patient needing my care. Rather, I felt that I should sit at her feet all day after anointing them with perfume. Being seen with such clear eyes of acceptance felt so good and so right. I was no longer the "blesser" but the blessed. And yet it is assumed that I am the one giving to the poor. What a mysterious twist of perspective as the kingdom next door broke into my world through Joan.

Another special presentation of God to me at this church is Alisa. She is a gangly six-footer with Down's Syndrome (a label that isn't really very helpful). She often comes up behind me, taps me on the shoulder, and wants to give me a hug. A hug for most of us is something we give with certain conditions attached. Usually, our relationship with the other person will determine what kind of hug can be given. Hugging someone of the opposite sex also needs to be approached differently than hugging someone of your own gender, especially in this age of caution about abuse. Age is also something to be mindful of, since hugging a child is different than hugging a brother on the battlefield. Unfortunately, these are necessary realities required to protect people's dignity and safety. Yet with Alisa, she shows no reservations in her affection. In fact, although I don't know her well, she seems very content to bury her face in my neck and remain there for extraordinarily long periods of time. Long arms wrapped around me, she stays close and still, like a bird safe in a down-filled nest, occasionally humming or laughing in my ear. She seems to know that she is safe when she is this close to me, and I sense that if I pulled away, it would be inappropriate somehow. The fact that she feels safe enough nuzzle in close to me without fear blesses me. I feel like I have been given something precious to protect and a special purpose to perform. Maybe this is how God feels when we tuck in close to him.

Robert is another, less affectionate, yet powerful ally in the arduous task of removing the scales from my eyes. He is an individual that I work with at a long-term care facility. He isn't particularly able to treat me with much tenderness at all. In fact, because his condition makes for a very tormented life, he cannot seem to treat himself with kindness either. When he gets upset, he often abuses himself to satisfy his sensory needs and to communicate his displeasure. This involves biting and hitting himself on his arms and legs, which often become raw and bloody. It is a very difficult thing to witness and often brings out despair in me. I become very angry at such a miserable condition and at my inability to fix it. After years of self-abuse, the skin on Robert's hands and arms has become thick and leathery. And because he likes to suck on his fingers to soothe himself, it is unpleasant to be within his reach. Yet when I allow compassion to move me and I come in close to him, Robert's hands often astound me. He won't often place his hands in mine, but when he does let them rest there, sometimes I see something beautiful. Are you familiar with those 3-D pictures that you have to stare at for a while until your brain reorients itself and the picture rises up off the page? When Robert's hands come into focus properly, I can see that they contain the image of God. In his gnarled, broken hands, self-abused and torn hands, hands weathered by deep anxiety, hands wet with the comfort of his own mouth, I see Christ's hands—hands that have not avoided the cost of love, hands that have refused to be snatched away even when bitten or burned.

In these rare moments when I give my imagination enough peace to see beyond the obvious, I find that my world changes. It changes, because when I see the image of God in Robert, I am no longer able to judge him by my own shallow prejudices, fears, and measurements of worth. When my view of him changes, my view of everything changes. For if God can be found in such lowly hands, he can be found anywhere, even in the hands of those I consider my enemies. Maybe I can even begin to see this beautiful image in myself, in my own hands and in my own damaged ways that I keep me far from God.

The thing about Joan, Alisa, and Robert—and the many other challenged individuals in my world—is that they expose me. This sounds negative, and it truly is when they reveal my indifference, impatience, anger, and fear. But they also expose me to who I really am. They call forward things in myself that I like. They give me an opportunity to be me… the real me. With them, I am free. They never respond to me with judgement, hatred or fear. Even Robert, in his torment, seldom strikes out at me. His anguish is nearly always directed inward. Their grace brings out my own, and I find that I like myself more when I am with them… especially when I live in the freedom of their seemingly instant and automatic forgiveness. Their holy task is to bring out the holy in me. But this, of course, is what all saints—both small "s" and big "S"saints—are to do.

I believe that my challenged friends are just the tip of the iceberg when it comes to seeing beyond the obvious. In them is hidden the promise of God to inhabit cracked jars of clay. Because of their ability to live authentically broken, the Jesus in them is more easily poured out than in those of us who are able and motivated to hide our pain. In many ways, I see these people as the hope for healing for all of us "normal" ones. For in the same way that we can see God manifest through their weakness, we can see him bring forth his power in our own unique weaknesses. I can see God in these people, because they let me get close enough to see him and to feel him in them. My hope is that we can develop our spiritual sight sufficiently to see each other in that same way. And I pray that the church would see those who dare to venture close to us as precious vessels of God's image—eyes that see Christ in the least of these.

Preface

Kissing the Leper

By Brad Jersak

There's somethin' wrong with the world today
I don't know what it is, something's wrong with our eyes

We're seeing things in a different way
And God knows it ain't his, it sure ain't no surprise

Aerosmith

This is how God inspired me, Brother Francis, to embark upon a life of penance. When I was in sin, the sight of lepers nauseated me beyond measure; but then God himself led me into their company, and I had pity on them. When I had once become acquainted with them, what had previously nauseated me became a source of spiritual and physical consolation for me. After that I did not wait long before leaving the world.

The Testament of St. Francis

K ISSING THE LEPER is a book about having eyes to see. Jesus once counseled us: *"Buy medicine for your eyes from me so you can see, really see"* (Revelation 3:18 MSG). *Kissing the Leper* is about getting our eyes repaired from religious and cultural prejudice so that we can see Jesus in others, especially those that our world discards as "the least." The title of this book was inspired by an encounter that Francis of Assisi had with Christ in a leper (recounted later in this preface). In that moment, his eyes were opened to the possibility of seeing and being Jesus among those who have traditionally been excluded from God's banqueting table. Somehow, when we turn away those we deem too sinful, too broken, too small or too poor, we expel Christ, himself, from our midst (as we'll see when we look at Matthew 25, our key text for this book. Cf. also 1 John 3:16-17). But when we welcome those cast out of society and the Church, we're also welcoming Jesus, whether we recognize him or not. Francis' conversion was brought about by him *seeing Jesus'* broken body in the decomposing body of the leper.

Further, in kissing the leper, Francis was also *being Jesus* to him. In the Apostle Paul's language, the love of Christ compelled him, both the love of Christ in Francis and his own love for Christ. Francis served and loved, yet it was truly Christ serving and loving the leper through him.

Finally, like the leper, Francis finds that by *meeting Jesus* through the "least of these," he, himself, is transformed. God's love often reaches out and touches us through surprising messengers, assaulting our prejudices by visiting us through modern day lepers and Samaritans whom we've judged as the least and the lost. Are we alert for these visitations?

Take note! The people in this book are *not* lepers. In God's eyes, they are *not* the least, *not* the lost. But the world, and too often the Church, has treated them that way. We need God's eyes to see them as he does. Herein, I will only use labels like *disabled* or *poor* or *bisexual* as a preface to removing those often libellous tags. Only as we know and love such marginalized people by name do we truly begin to see and know them as Jesus does.

What follows in this preface are three versions of Francis' story, each revealing important details about his encounter. Together, they set the stage for such encounters in our own lives.

I

One day, the man we now know as St. Francis was riding across the valley toward Assisi, and neared a little hospital for lepers, where he had often stopped with gifts of money. His heart was full of sorrow for these sufferers from the most terrible of all diseases, and he thought: "I will go in today and leave something for them." Outside the gate of the hospital, crouched against the wall in the sunshine, one of the lepers sat to ask alms of passing travellers. The poor man was covered with sores, and revolting to look upon. At sight of him, Francis felt a sickening sense of disgust and horror. He drew his purse hastily from his belt and, tossing it to the leper, rode on as fast as his horse could carry him, trying to forget the face that had been raised to his. Suddenly, like an arrow, the thought struck him: "That man, also, is my brother, and I have despised him!" The rider dropped his rein, and the horse went slowly along the rough road between the olive orchards. Francis was both ashamed and disappointed. He said to himself: "My purse was an insult, for I gave it without love, and with more scorn than pity."

The spring sun was high and hot; the sky was cloudless; not a shadow lay on the vast, bare height of Monte Subasio. At a fountain beside the road some women were washing. They sang as they worked and, at the end of the long fountain basin, a group of children shouted with laughter, dipping their little hands into the cold water, and splashing one another merrily. All the world seemed happy in the sunshine, and, by contrast, the misery of the poor leper seemed the greater. At the sound of hoofs, the songs and laughter ceased and all turned to look at the newcomer; but, to the surprise of everyone, the horseman wheeled swiftly about, and clattered back in the direction from which he had come. "Who is he?" one woman asked of another. "Only that young Bernardone, the merchant's son," was the answer; "people say that he has gone mad." Then an old, bent woman spoke: "Mad or not, he has a kind heart. It was his gold that kept my poor Giovanni alive last winter. I wish that more of the rich folk were mad like him."

Francis heard nothing. He rode fast across the valley toward the little hospital. He had not been gone ten minutes, and the leper, scarcely recovered from his surprise at the generous gift he had received, was creeping to the gate with his treasure. He moved slowly, as if in pain. Francis sprang from his horse, and, kneeling in the dusty road, he lifted the leper's hand to his lips and kissed it, as he had been taught to kiss the hand of a bishop or a prince. It is likely that the leper was as greatly puzzled as the beggar in the porch of St. Peter's had been, but Francis Bernardone was not mad. Instead, he had learned, through his own failure and shame, a lesson that some men never learn; for, "though I give all my gifts to feed the poor, and have not love, it is nothing." From that spring morning, at the gate of the leper hospital, until the day of his death, Francis of Assisi never met the man who was too filthy, or too loathsome, or even too wicked, for him to love.[1]

II

Among all the awful miseries of this world Francis had a natural horror of lepers, and one day as he was riding his horse near Assisi he met a leper on the road. He felt terrified and revolted, but not wanting to transgress God's command and break the sacrament of his word, he dismounted from his horse and ran to kiss him. As the leper stretched out his hand, expecting something, he received both money and a kiss. Francis immediately mounted his horse and although the field was wide open, without any obstruction, when he looked around he could not see the leper anywhere. Filled with joy and wonder at this event, within a few days he deliberately tried to do something similar. He made his way to the houses of the lepers and, giving money to each, he also gave a kiss on the hand and mouth. Thus he took the bitter for the sweet (Proverbs 27: 7) and courageously prepared to carry out the rest.[2]

---

[1] Sophie Jewett, *God's Troubadour, The Story of Saint Francis of Assisi* (New York, NY: Thomas Y. Crowell Company, 1910) 10.

[2] Regis J. Armstrong, William J. Short, and J. A. Wayne Hellmann, (eds.), *Francis of Assisi: Early Documents* (St. Bonaventure, NY: The Franciscan Institute, St. Bonaventure University, 2002) 2 Celano 9.

III

From then on he clothed himself with a spirit of poverty, a sense of humility, and an eagerness for intimate piety. For previously not only had association with lepers horrified him greatly, so too did even gazing upon them from a distance. But, now because of Christ crucified, who according to the text of the prophet appeared despised as a leper (Isaiah 53: 3), he, in order to despise himself completely, showed deeds of humility and humanity to lepers with a gentle piety.[3]

A Franciscan Summary

Francis cultivated a mystical and deeply personal relationship with the person of Jesus Christ. This relationship was so profound, that for the last three years of his life, he bore the marks of the Crucified Jesus in his own body, known as the stigmata. He was in fact the first person in Christian history to have received this extraordinary gift. Thus, when he related to his fellow human beings, it was through the eyes and heart of Jesus. When he embraced that leper on the road near Assisi, it was not only a hideous leper whom he kissed but also the very person of Jesus, incarnate in the leper. For Francis, Jesus was present in every human person, but particularly in the poor and outcasts.[4]

---

[3] *Major Life of St. Francis by St. Bonaventure,* I, 6. Ibid.

[4] Franciscan Friars–Province of the Holy Spirit, "Francis and Nature" (accessed 25 Jan., 2006) available from http://www.franciscans.org.au/ spirituality.

Part 1

Seeing Jesus
in the Least of These

Benedict XVI: *On Christian Love*[1]

God is love, and he who abides in love abides in God, and God abides in him" (1 John 4:16). These words from the First Letter of John express with remarkable clarity the heart of the Christian faith: the Christian image of God and the resulting image of mankind and its destiny. In the same verse, Saint John also offers a kind of summary of the Christian life:

We have come to believe in God's love: in these words the Christian can express the fundamental decision of his life. Being a Christian is not the result of an ethical choice or a lofty idea, but the encounter with an event, a person, which gives life a new horizon and a decisive direction...

Love of neighbour is thus shown to be possible in the way proclaimed by the Bible, by Jesus. It consists in the very fact that, in God and with God, I love even the person whom I do not like or even know. This can only take place on the basis of an intimate encounter with God, an encounter which has become a communion of will, even affecting my feelings. Then I learn to look on this other person not simply with my eyes and my feelings, but from the perspective of Jesus Christ. His friend is my friend... Seeing with the eyes of Christ, I can give to others much more than their outward necessities: I can give them the look of love which they crave...

The Christian programme—the programme of the Good Samaritan, the programme of Jesus—is "a heart which sees". This heart sees where love is needed and acts accordingly.

---

[1] Pope Benedict XVI, *Encyclical Letter: On Christian Love* (accessed 28 Feb., 2006) available from http://www.vatican.va/holy_father/benedict_xvi/encyclicals/documents/hf_ben-xvi_enc_20051225_deus-caritas-est_en.html.

1

"What you did to the least of these..."

By Brad Jersak

The Judgment of the Sheep and the Goats

When the Son of Man comes in his glory, and all the angels with him, he will sit on his throne in heavenly glory. All the nations will be gathered before him, and he will separate the people one from another as a shepherd separates the sheep from the goats. He will put the sheep on his right and the goats on his left.

Then the King will say to those on his right, "Come, you who are blessed by my Father; take your inheritance, the kingdom prepared for you since the creation of the world. For I was hungry and you gave me something to eat, I was thirsty and you gave me something to drink, I was a stranger and you invited me in, I needed clothes and you clothed me, I was sick and you looked after me, I was in prison and you came to visit me."

Then the righteous will answer him, "Lord, when did we see him hungry and feed you, or thirsty and give you something to drink? When did we see you a stranger and invite you in, or needing clothes and clothe you? When did we see you sick or in prison and go to visit you?"

The King will reply, "I tell you the truth, whatever you did for one of the least of these brothers of mine, you did for me."

Then he will say to those on his left, "Depart from me, you who are cursed, into the eternal fire prepared for the devil and his angels. For I was hungry and you gave me nothing to eat, I was thirsty and you gave me nothing to drink, I was a stranger and you did not invite me in, I needed clothes and you did not clothe me, I was sick and in prison and you did not look after me."

They also will answer, "Lord, when did we see you hungry or thirsty or a stranger or needing clothes or sick or in prison, and did not help you?"

He will reply, "I tell you the truth, whatever you did not do for one of the least of these, you did not do for me."

Then they will go away to eternal punishment, but the righteous to eternal life.

Matthew 25:31–46 (NIV)

● ● ● ● ● ●

THE MYSTERY AND DILEMMA OF JESUS' lone description of Judgment Day revolves around two groups of questions that potentially change the way we see God, humankind, and how we "do life."

Group 1: *How is it that we see Jesus in others? Why would this especially be true of the least among us? How is it possible to see Jesus even in the so-called "unbeliever"? To whom does "these brothers of mine" refer?*

Traditionally, we've made a case for seeing Christ in others based on God's image. In Genesis 1:26, God says, "Let us make man[kind] in our image and after our likeness." Whatever the image of God really is and no matter how it was tarnished through our fall from Eden, most Christians agree that God's image remains in *every* living person, giving them intrinsic dignity and worth. On that basis, you might see Christ in anyone, since *he is the image* of the invisible God (Col. 1:15). It's a good, standard theological answer.

Similarly, the prologue to John's gospel may suggest that the light of Christ is freely given to and shines in *everyone*: "That was the true Light which gives light to every man coming into the world" (1 John 1:9 NKJV).

However, as I continued to press God on this in prayer, I believe he offered a complimentary truth; one that explains why we might specifically see Jesus Christ—and not just something vaguely "godlike"—in everyone. This includes the nonbeliever and also (especially) the poor and broken. I sensed the Lord saying something like this:

> You can see me in all people, not because they become Christians, but because I became human—human with a capital 'H' [Cf. Romans 5, where Christ came as the second Adam].

When the Word became flesh (John 1:14), I identified with every man, woman, and child on the planet... And I especially identified with the sufferings of the least of these. They are my little brothers and sisters, not because of their creed or confession, but because of my humanity.

At the Cross, in co-suffering love, I identified with them in every way. Now I invite them to come to the Cross and identify with me in every way, especially with my love. That love will look like Matthew 25.

You do not see Christ in 'unbelievers' because they become Christians.

You see Christ in them and in everyone because he became Human with a capital 'H.'

This is the essence of the incarnation and the meaning of the Cross (what we call "atonement," i.e. how the Cross saves us). Christ emptied Himself, embracing all that we are—trials and temptations, poverty, suffering, and death—to identify with us by becoming one of us. In giving himself to all humankind, he invites us, in turn, to identify with him by 1) leaving our guilt, shame, and egos to die at the Cross, and 2) saying *Yes* to his call to a new life empowered by God's love and mercy.

Such far-reaching, sacrificial love suggests that the Lord wants us to treat everyone, especially the lowly, with the care and respect that we would have for Christ himself. God esteems them—indeed, he lives with them—in a special way. As God said through the prophet Isaiah,

> I live in a high and holy place,
> but also with him who is contrite and lowly in spirit,
> to revive the spirit of the lowly
> and to revive the heart of the contrite.
> (Isaiah 57:14–15)

Clothing himself with humanity, we see Christ fulfilling this promise to be in and among all people, and especially near to those most likely to be overlooked or discarded.

Group 2: *How is it that in Matthew 25, Christ's criterion for entry into the kingdom seems to be compassion rather than faith? The judgment looks to be based on how we treat him in the least rather than by simple belief in him (John 3:16) or by "grace through faith, and not by good deeds" (Ephesians 2:8–10). Is Christ preaching a "works message" that reverts to salvation through our own efforts?*

Matthew 25 actually transcends the old works versus grace debate by suggesting something that goes beyond such either/or thinking.

First, we must affirm that entry into God's kingdom does *not* come by works-righteousness or from trying to be good enough for God. According to Paul, dedication to law-keeping and the proliferation of good deeds won't cut it (Galatians 3). He says, "For it is by grace you have been saved, through faith—and this not from yourselves, it is the gift of God—not by works, so that no one can boast" (Ephesians 2:8–9).

Jesus, too, warned us not to depend on the notches we've carved on our spiritual belts,

> "Many will say to me on that day, 'Lord, Lord, did we not prophesy in your name, and in your name drive out demons and perform many miracles?' Then I will tell them plainly, 'I never knew you. Away from me, you evildoers!'" (Matthew 7:22–23)

On the other hand, neither are we justified by cheap grace or an "easy-believism" in which the magical "sinner's prayer" grants us our barcode for heaven's check-in.[1] St. James warns,

> Thus also faith by itself, if it does not have works, is dead... You believe that there is one God. You do well. Even the demons believe—and tremble! (James 2:17, 19 NKJV)

Nor is Jesus unconcerned with how we live. Cognitive belief in his name or mental assent to the right creed misses the point. God's grace does *not* negate Jesus' call to take up your cross and follow him. Faith in the finished work of Christ does not replace his commandment to love (as if obeying him is legalistic).

> Likewise every good tree bears good fruit, but a bad tree bears bad fruit. A good tree cannot bear bad fruit, and a bad tree cannot bear good fruit. Every tree that does not bear good fruit is cut down and thrown into the fire. Thus, by their fruit you will recognize them.

---

[1] Cf. Dallas Willard, *The Divine Conspiracy* (San Francisco: Harper San Francisco, 1999) 36ff.

Not everyone who says to me, 'Lord, Lord,' will enter the kingdom of heaven, but only he who does the will of my Father who is in heaven. (Matthew 7:17–21 NIV)

There's a saying we use these days to remind people to slow down and *just be*: "Be a human being, not a human doing." But when we say that, though we only intend to caution against drivenness, we actually recreate the false binary established during the Reformation that pits faith against works. God calls us to emerge from that trap into a third way: NOT as human doings. NOR even as human beings. BUT as *humans loving.* Jesus came to make us fully human once again. He is graciously rehumanizing mankind with a transforming *love-righteousness.* The law he writes on our hearts is the royal law of love. *Living* faith says an active, life-altering *Yes* to that work of grace. It requires us to follow Jesus into practical, transforming participation in his kingdom agenda of love. It looks like compassion, mercy, peacemaking, and justice. It looks like Matthew 25.

"There is no entry into the Kingdom apart from the Great Moral Imperative."[2] I.e. I really must love the Lord my God with all my heart, soul, mind, and strength and I must love my neighbor as myself (Luke 10:25–28). For in loving my neighbor, I'll find that I am loving Jesus. With "born again eyes," I will find that I am both seeing and entering the Kingdom of Love.

---

[2] Archbishop Lazar Puhalo, "The Oil of Humanity: The Great Moral Imperative Restated," *Clarion: Journal of Spirituality and Justice,* Vol. 5, Nov. 2005 (All Souls, All Saints) 5–8.

God is in the slums, in the cardboard boxes where the poor play house. God is in the silence of a mother who has infected her child with a virus that will end both their lives… God is in the cries heard under the rubble of war. God is in the debris of wasted opportunity and lives, and God is with us if we are with them.

Bono
National Prayer Breakfast, Washington, 2006

2

"You know me, Raymond..."

By Ray Loewen

O N A FRIGID SUNDAY evening in February 2001, ten people from Altona, MB, Canada drove into the city of Winnipeg to participate in an evening of praise and worship at the Vineyard Church. The church was located just off of Main Street, an area often busy with glue-sniffers, prostitutes, and the poorest folks in the city. We parked our cars in front of the church and gathered inside for an incredible time of worship. After the service, while returning to our cars, we noticed a couple coming down the street. She kept walking, not really paying attention to us. But the mangy looking man stopped and began to plead for some money.

"Hey buddy. Got any change? I need some money," he slurred. Some in our group, perhaps nervous, made for their cars, but I moved toward him, fumbling in my jacket pockets for change. As I got closer, I was greeted by the overpowering smell of alcohol and glue on his breath. In the icy weather, he had drooled over his scraggly beard, which was now matted and frozen over with saliva icicles. He kept pressing, now more insistent, "Hurry up, she's getting away," referring to his companion who was disappearing down the street. I still remember fumbling for change and making excuses about not having much money to give...

At that point he looked directly at me and said in a clear, firm voice: *"You know me, Raymond. Hurry up and give me some money."*

As you can imagine, the rational side of my brain went a little nuts. I was hit by a barrage of thoughts: Why did you call me Raymond? Nobody has called me that since I was a kid! And I always hated that name! What do you mean you know me? I don't know you! We have never met! You *can't* know me! Okay, this is just a coincidence. He picked a name, and it just so happens that of the two hundred people leaving the church, he picked mine! He must have meant that *his* name was Raymond. He must have been trying to say, "You know me. *I'm* Raymond."

Again, just a coincidence? We just happened to share the same name and be the two people who would face off on a cold winter night in the north end of Winnipeg?

While the analytical side of my brain was screaming along at warp speed trying in vain to rationalize what had just happened, my intuitive side began to recall Jesus' words in the

Gospel of Matthew where he describes the judgment of the sheep and goats. I could see the story in my mind's eye even while the man held out his hand.

Eugene Peterson's *The Message* tells the story of Matthew 25 this way:

> When he finally arrives, blazing in beauty and all his angels with him, the Son of Man will take his place on his glorious throne. Then all the nations will be arranged before him and he will sort the people out, much as a shepherd sorts out sheep and goats, putting sheep to his right and goats to his left… then he will turn to the goats, the ones on his left, and say, "Get out worthless goats. You're good for nothing but the fires of hell. And why?
>
> Because: I was hungry and you gave me no meal. I was thirsty and you gave me no drink. I was homeless and you gave me no bed. I was shivering and you gave me no clothes. Sick and in prison, and you never visited."
>
> Then those goats are going to say, "Master what are you talking about? When did we see you hungry, shivering or sick or in prison and didn't help?"
>
> He will answer them, "I'm telling the solemn truth—whenever you failed to do one of these things to someone who was being overlooked or ignored, that was me—you failed to do it to me."

That night on the cold streets of Winnipeg, I saw myself standing before God's judgment throne and hearing Jesus say, "Remember that night just off Main Street? *I even called you by name,* and still you ignored me…"

In that epiphany, I discovered God's purpose for me. By day, I sell used cars in Southern Manitoba. But God's purpose in me had a lot more to do with Jesus' challenge to meet him on the road in the least and the lost—and a lot less to do with getting more consumers on the road in cars and trucks.

• • • • • •

Several months later, in September 2001, I made my first trip to El Salvador as part of the Mennonite Central Committee's (MCC) *Build a Village* project, which involves raising money and building homes for earthquake victims. By then I had helped prepare two other "work and learn" teams but had never gone myself. My plan was to go to El Salvador and live out Matthew 25. I was going to help someone in need; to provide a home for a family that did not have one. Two days after arriving in the country I became sick, first with an upset stomach from the food or the water, then on the second evening, with a severe pain in my back which I had never experienced before (which turned out to be a kidney stone attack).

I was lying on a mat on the cement floor of the community centre feeling miserable and a little sorry for myself. I was asking God some "Why?" questions, as in "Why me?" and "Why now?" After all, he knew how I had longed to come to El Salvador to live out his words from Matthew 25. Couldn't we arrange for this pain to come back in a few weeks after my return to Canada? Everything was backwards. Others were bringing *me* food and drink; visiting me when *I* was sick; coming to pray with *me* for healing! People were coming to care for me and feed me and love me!

On the second morning, it hit me: I *was* living out the verses in Matthew 25! But I had expected to live them as the "giver." Now I was experiencing them as the "receiver." I had never expected to learn it this way, but God used my illness to confirm the importance of the Matthew 25 kind of compassion:

Then the King will say to those on his right, "Enter, you who are blessed by my Father! Take what's coming to you in this kingdom. It's been ready for you since the world's foundation. And here's why: I was hungry and you fed me, I was thirsty and you gave me a drink, I was homeless and you gave me a room, I was shivering and you gave me clothes, I was sick and you stopped to visit, I was in prison and you came to me." Then those 'sheep' are going to say, "Master, what are you talking about? When did we ever see you hungry and feed you, thirsty and give you a drink? And when did we ever see you sick or in prison and come to you?" Then the King will say, "I'm telling the solemn truth: Whenever you did one of these things to someone overlooked or ignored, that was me—you did it to me." (Matthew 25:34–40 MSG)

3

Mr. "Thelord"

by Marshall Rosenberg[1]

I ONCE ASKED my uncle Julius how he had developed such a remarkable capacity to give compassionately. He seemed honored by my question, which he pondered before replying, "I've been blessed with good teachers." When I asked who these were, he recalled, "Your grandmother was the best teacher I had. You lived with her when she was already ill, so you didn't know what she was really like. For example, did your mother ever tell you about the time during the Depression when she brought a tailor and his wife and two children to live with her for three years, after he lost his house and business?" I remembered the story well. It left a deep impression when my mother first told it

---

[1] This essay originally appeared in Marshall B. Rosenberg, *Nonviolent Communication: A Language of Life* (Encinatas, CA: PuddleDancer Press, 2003) 193-195. Used by permission.

to me because I could never figure out where Grandmother had found space for the tailor's family when she was raising nine children of her own in a modest-sized house!

Uncle Julius recollected my grandmother's compassion in a few more anecdotes, all of which I had heard as a child. Then he asked, "Surely your mother told you about Jesus."

"About who?"

"Jesus."

"No, she never told me about Jesus."

The story about Jesus was the final precious gift I received from my uncle before he died. It's a true story of a time when a man came to my grandmother's back door asking for some food. This wasn't unusual. Although Grandmother was very poor, the entire neighborhood knew that she would feed anyone who showed up at her door. The man had a beard and wild scraggly black hair; his clothes were ragged and he wore a cross around his neck fashioned out of branches tied with rope. My grandmother invited him into her kitchen for some food, and while he was eating she asked his name.

"My name is Jesus," he replied.

"Do you have a last name?" she inquired.

"I am Jesus the Lord." (My grandmother's English wasn't too good. Another Uncle, Isador, later told me he had come into the kitchen while the man was eating and Grandmother had introduced the stranger as "Mr. Thelord.")

As he continued to eat, my grandmother asked where he lived.

"I don't have a home."

"Well, where are you going to stay tonight? It's cold."

"I don't know."

"Would you like to stay here?" she offered.

He stayed seven years.

When it came to communicating nonviolently, my grandmother was a natural. She didn't think of what this man "was." If she did, she probably would have judged him as crazy and gotten rid of him. No, she thought in terms of what people feel and what they need. If they're hungry, feed them. If they're without a roof over their head, give them a place to sleep.

My grandmother loved to dance, and my mother remembers her saying often, "Never walk when you can dance." And thus I end this book on a language of compassion with a song about my grandmother, who spoke and lived the language of Nonviolent Communication.

One day a man named Jesus
came around to my grandmother's door.
He asked for a little food,
she gave him more.

He said he was Jesus the Lord;
she didn't check him out with Rome.
He stayed for several years,
as did many without a home.

It was in her Jewish way,
she taught me what Jesus had to say.
It was in her Jewish way,
she taught me what Jesus had to say.

And that's: "Feed the hungry, heal the sick,
then take a rest.
Never walk when you can dance;
make your home a cozy nest."

It was in her Jewish way,
she taught me what Jesus had to say.
In her precious way,
she taught me what Jesus had to say.

4

Changing Jesus' Diapers

Collected by Brad Jersak

At the end of our lives, we will not be judged by how many diplomas we have received, how much money we have made or how many great things we have done. We will be judged by 'I was hungry and you gave me to eat. I was naked and you clothed me. I was homeless and you took me in.' Hungry not only for bread—but hungry for love. Naked not only for clothing—but naked of human dignity and respect. Homeless not only for want of a room of bricks—but homeless because of rejection. This is Christ in distressing disguise.[1]

Mother Teresa

---

[1] EWTN: Global Catholic Network, *A Vocation of Service* (accessed 25 Jan. 2006) available from http://www.ewtn.com/motherteresa/vocation.htm.

MOTHER TERESA OF CALCUTTA, late founder of the Missionaries for Charity, was a remarkable little woman with God-graced eyes. Her heart for the poor and sick derived from a vision of Christ in each of them, regardless of caste, gender or faith. I believe her ability to see Jesus in the least of these was more than a personal philosophy; it was her source of divine strength through many decades. It literally energized her. As I have collected statements by or about Teresa, I see this recurring message as the theme of her life. Herein is a sampling.

● ● ● ● ● ●

Responding to Christ's words to her in prayer, Mother Teresa founded the Missionaries of Charity in 1952. For over forty-five years, she continued her selfless work, developing homes around the world for drug addicts, prostitutes, battered women, AIDS victims, and orphans. Her zeal and works of mercy knew no bounds. The Missionaries of Charity grew from twelve sisters to thousands, serving the poorest of the poor in 450 centers. Mother Teresa died at eighty-seven on September 5, 1997. Her work lives on.

The Missionaries of Charity are contemplative and conquering. Everything is for Christ, through Christ, and in Christ... Day in and day out, they persevere, praying four hours, sleeping six, and serving the rest. They are tough and holy. Their deep prayer life, centered on the body and blood of Jesus in the Eucharist, nourishes their soul, giving supernatural strength.

To the sisters, the neglected poor man is nothing less than Jesus crying for recognition and love, Jesus in need of food, Jesus without a home. They see in the face of each and every poor person the face of Jesus. They change the diapers of

Jesus, cook and provide meals for Jesus, wash the handi-
capped Jesus, and much more. They are his servants.[2]

Peter Reynolds

Tell them that we are not here for the work, we are here for
Jesus. All we do is for him. We are first of all religious; we
are not social workers, not teachers, not nurses, or doctors,
we are religious sisters. We serve Jesus in the poor. We nurse
him, feed him, clothe him, visit him, comfort him in the
poor, the abandoned, the sick, the orphans, the dying. But all
we do, our prayers, our work, our suffering is for Jesus. Our
life has no other reason or motivation. This is a point many
people do not understand. I serve Jesus twenty-four hours
a day, whatever I do is for him. And he gives me strength.
I love him in the poor and the poor in him. But always the
Lord comes first.[3]

Teresa of Calcutta

At this time of prayer I am pleased to recall our very dear sister, Mother Teresa of Calcutta... Missionary of Charity. Her
mission began every day, before dawn, in the presence of the
Eucharist. In the silence of contemplation, Mother Teresa of
Calcutta heard the echo of Jesus' cry on the cross: "I thirst".

---

[2] Peter Reynolds, "Mother Teresa, Her Sisters, and Georgetown
University: Serving Jesus in the Poor," *AD2000*, Vol. 18, No. 5,
June 2005, 10.

[3] Mother Teresa in conversation with Edward Le Joly, 1977 (accessed
25 Jan. 2006) available from http://www.go2nepal.com/mt.html.

This cry, received in the depths of her heart, spurred her to seek out Jesus in the poor, the abandoned and the dying on the streets of Calcutta and to all the ends of the earth. Dear brothers and sisters, this sister, universally known as the Mother of the poor, leaves an eloquent example for everyone, believer and non-believer. She leaves us the witness of God's love, which she accepted and which transformed her life into a total gift to her brothers and sisters. She leaves us the witness of contemplation which becomes love, of love which becomes contemplation. The works she accomplished speak for themselves and show the people of our time that lofty meaning of life which unfortunately seems often to be lost.[4]

Pope John Paul II

Jesus is the Hungry–to be fed.
Jesus is the Thirsty–to be satiated.
Jesus is the Naked–to be clothed.
Jesus is the Homeless–to be taken in.
Jesus is the Sick–to be healed.
Jesus is the Lonely–to be loved.
Jesus is the Unwanted–to be wanted.
Jesus is the Leper–to wash his wounds.
Jesus is the Beggar–to give him a smile.
Jesus is the Drunkard–to listen to him.
Jesus is the Mental–to protect him.
Jesus is the Little One–to embrace him.
Jesus is the Blind–to lead him.

---

[4] Pope John Paul II, *"Sunday Angelus: On Mother Teresa," EL' Osserva-tore Romano,* Sept. 10, 1997 (Weekly Edition in English) 1.

Jesus is the Dumb–to speak for him.
Jesus is the Crippled–to walk with him.
Jesus is the Drug Addict–to befriend him.
Jesus is the Prostitute–to remove from danger and
befriend her.
Jesus is the Prisoner–to be visited.
Jesus is the Old–to be served.[5]

Teresa of Calcutta

The key to understanding Mother Teresa and the Missionaries
of Charity is the sacredness with which they treat all people
and their humble way of carrying out their work. To the
Missionaries of Charity, Jesus is present in everyone they
meet whether it is a young volunteer from New Jersey or an
old Muslim woman starved and half-eaten by rats and worms,
or the deformed infant just born and left in a garbage heap.
Christ is present in everyone, but most especially in the poorest of the poor. From the very beginning, Mother Teresa and
her order reached out to treat each person they encountered as
they would Jesus Christ. Thus, they performed each task for
the benefit of the poor as they would do it for Christ. In other
words, it is Jesus' diapers they wash, his meals they prepare,
his ailing body they tend, and his hand being held.[6]

Journalist Mary Poplin

---

[5] Mother Teresa, *No Greater Love,* ed. by Becky Benenate and Joseph
Durepos (Novato, CA: New World Library, 1997) 89.

[6] Mary Poplin, "No Humanitarian: A Portrait of Mother Teresa,"
Commonweal, Vol. 124, December 19, 1997 (accessed 25 Jan. 2006)
available from http://www.findarticles.com/p/articles/mi_m1252/is_
n22_v124/ai_20314571.

It is not enough for us to say: 'I love God, but I do not love my neighbor.' Saint John says that you are a liar if you say you love God and you don't love your neighbor. How can you love God whom you do not see, if you do not love your neighbor whom you see, whom you touch, with whom you live? And so this is very important for us to realize that *love, to be true, has to hurt.*[7]

Teresa of Calcutta

To be able to love one another, we must pray much, for prayer gives a clean heart and a clean heart can see God in our neighbor. If now we have no peace, it is because we have forgotten how to see God in one another. *If each person saw God in his neighbor, do you think we would need guns and bombs?*

We do not think every time we are talking to someone, "Jesus is in that person." In the parable in our Gospel the people did not think either of the presence of God in those around them. That is why in the parable both those to the left of the Son of Man and those on his right say, "Lord when did we see you hungry or thirsty or a stranger or naked or sick or in prison?"[8]

Teresa of Calcutta

---

[7] Mother Teresa, *Nobel Lecture,* Oslo, Dec. 11, 1979 (accessed 25 Jan. 2006) available from http://gos.sbc.edu/m/teresanobel.html.

[8] Mother Teresa, *Letter to the People of Albania*, April 1997 (accessed 25 Jan. 2006) available from http://www.newalbaniangeneration.com/motherteresaletter.html.

True evangelism, based on the example of Jesus, does not suggest the "missionary zeal" of self-righteous proselytizers. It implies, on the contrary, the kind of all-embracing universality evident in Mother Teresa's prayer: *"May God break my heart so completely that the whole world falls in."* Not just fellow nuns, Catholics, Calcuttans, Indians. The whole world. It gives me pause to realize that, were such a prayer said by me and answered by God, I would afterward possess a heart so open that even hate-driven zealots would fall inside.[9]

David James Duncan

> # Jesus, my patient, how sweet it is to serve you.
> ## Mother Teresa

Dearest Lord, may I see you today and everyday in the person of your sick and while nursing them minister unto you.

Though you hide yourself behind the unattractive disguise of the irritable, the exacting, the unreasonable, may I still recognise you and say: *"Jesus, my patient, how sweet it is to serve you."*

Lord, give me this seeing faith, then my work will never be

---

[9] David James Duncan, "In Defence of Truth," *Synearth* (accessed 25 Jan. 2006) available from http://news.synearth.net/2005/07/18.

monotonous. I will ever find joy in humouring the fancies and gratifying the wishes of all poor sufferers.

O beloved sick, how double dear you are to me, when you personify Christ; and what a privilege of mine to be allowed to tend you.

Sweetest Lord, make me appreciative of the dignity of my high vocation and its many responsibilities. Never permit me to disgrace it by giving way to coldness, unkindness or impatience.

And O God, while you are Jesus, my patient, deign also to be to me, a patient Jesus, bearing with my faults, looking only to my intention which is to love and serve you in the person of each of your sick.

Lord increase my faith, bless my efforts and work, now and for ever more.[10]

Mother Teresa

---

[10] Mother Teresa, "Daily Prayer: Jesus My Patient," *Moments by God–Serenity* (accessed 2 Feb. 2006) available at http://www.tbihome.org/gallery/beckyfromtexas/gallery4.html.

5

Adam

By Henri Nouwen[1]

*The late Henri Nouwen worked with Adam, a person with severe
disabilities, at Dayspring (one of the L'arche communities) in
Richmond Hill, Ontario. The story of Adam, completed just weeks
before Henri Nouwen's death, describes Nouwen's understanding of
the Gospel in the context of the least of these.*

A S I THINK ABOUT this first part of Adam's life I cannot
avoid seeing a close parallel to Jesus' home life. Jesus did
not come in power and might. He came dressed in weakness. The
greatest part of his life was hidden, sharing the human condition
as a baby, a young child, a struggling adolescent, and a maturing
adult. Adam's hidden life, like the life of Jesus of Nazareth, was

---

[1] Originally published in Henri Nouwen, *Adam: God's Beloved*
(Maryknoll, NY: Orbis Books, 1997) 141–142. Used by permission.

an unseen preparation for the time of his ministry to many people, even though neither he nor his parents looked on it that way.

I am not saying that Adam was a second Jesus. But I am saying that because of the vulnerability of Jesus we can see Adam's extremely vulnerable life as a life of utmost spiritual significance. Adam did not have unique heroic virtues: he did not excel in anything that newspapers write about. But I am convinced that Adam was chosen to witness to God's love through his brokenness. To say this is not to romanticize him or to be sentimental. Adam was, like all of us, a limited person, more limited than most, and unable to express himself in words. But he was also a whole person and a blessed man. In his weakness he became a unique instrument of God's grace. He became a revelation of Christ among us.

Adam possessed an inner light that was radiant. It was of God. He had few distractions, few attachments, and few ambitions to fill his inner space. Therefore, Adam did not have to practice the spiritual disciplines to become empty for God. His so-called "disability" gifted him with it. For him God was never the subject of an intellectual or emotional search. Like Jesus, his belovedness, his likeness to God, his mission of peace could be acknowledged only by those who were willing to welcome him as one sent by God.

Most people saw Adam as a disabled person who had little to give and who was a burden to his family, his community, and to society at large. And as long as he was seen that way, his truth was hidden. What was not received was not given.

But Adam's parents loved him simply because he was Adam. Yes, they recognized and loved him for himself. Without awareness they also welcomed him as one sent to us by God in utter vulnerability to be an instrument of God's blessing. That vision of him changes everything quite radically because then Adam emerges as someone, as special, as a wonderful, gifted, child of promise.

6

Eve

By Brad Jersak and Eve

E VE IS NOT YOUR TYPICAL five-year-old. There is nothing ordinary about her or her story. That's because Eve is a fully functional dissociative part of a very fragmented adult woman.[1] In other words, Eve appears to be one of many child personas all living within Janice (not her real name), a lady in her forties who experienced extreme trauma throughout her childhood and adolescence. To cope with life, Janice developed

---

[1] "Recently considered rare and mysterious psychiatric curiosities, Dissociative Identity Disorder (DID) (previously known as Multiple Personality Disorder-MPD) and other Dissociative Disorders are now understood to be fairly common effects of severe trauma in early childhood, most typically extreme, repeated physical, sexual, and/or emotional abuse." The Sydran Institute, *Dissociative Disorders,* (accessed 25 Jan. 2006) available at http://www.sidran.org/didbr.html.

the unconscious ability to create internal parts that carry her worst memories, store the bulk of her pain, and take on jobs in order to bring a semblance of internal order to her life. This is how Eve came to be.

Of course, before she met Jesus, Eve's idea of order was much different than ours. It involved a loyalty to demons who would empower her to punish Janice by cutting her with a knife whenever Janice did things to disrupt her inner system. All hell broke loose when Janice became a Christian.

Eve really believed herself to be pure evil—that no one could love her because all she was and all she knew was darkness. She had a filthy mouth and a mocking hatred for Jesus and anyone who loved him. Her self-perception as raw evil was confirmed even more when Christians identified her as a demon and tried to cast her out. The problem is, you can't cast out part of someone's soul. And, unlike a demon, Eve does not have to submit to deliverance ministers or even to Jesus, because she has a human will. In fact, such deliverance can become spiritual abuse, which only drives dissociated personality parts like Eve even deeper.

For a five-year-old, Eve was very powerful. She could send Janice into an unconscious state for hours with no recollection of what had occurred. Janice would "come to," finding new scars all over her arms and profane e-mails that Eve had sent to threaten her best friends. Bedtime was worse, with vivid nightly sexual assaults by invisible abusers, witnessed by her husband.

That's about the time I met Eve. I saw Janice trying to

bury herself into the corner of a church wall, and the Lord let me see what was happening. When she found her way back to the safety of a lovely support couple, I asked Janice if she'd let me give her a hug. Even through her fear and rejection issues, Janice nodded. When I have no adequate prayers to pray and no real hope of fixing anything, the love of God can be communicated in a hug even past the hardest heart. I silently prayed that Jesus would fill my arms with his love. After she received the "Jesus-hug," I looked in Janice's face, but I saw Eve's eyes. The hatred was so intense that I can understand why others mistook her for a demon. But I wasn't looking at a demon. I was looking at a miracle waiting to happen. I knew in my heart that I was looking at an angry, little girl who was just trying to do what she thought was her job. Her anger was a weapon forged to protect her, not that this worked very well. But I also sensed that little Eve had snuck part of that Jesus-hug for herself. I asked Jesus to fill my eyes with his mercy so that she could see that Jesus both knew her and loved her. I'm not her counselor, pastor or doctor, but in that moment, I became Eve's first friend.

It took a long time, and there were serious mishaps along the way, but little by little, Eve came to know Jesus for herself. Skipping the details of that stormy process, let me bring you up to speed. With Janice's permission, Eve (now her dear friend) wrote the following testimony of what it's like for her to know Jesus. Incidentally, if you happen to believe that all dissociated parts are demons, please listen carefully to this one. It may save others a great deal of pain (which is my agenda in sharing this).

• • • • • •

Hi Bradley,

So… You asked me about good 'ol Jesus!! Hee hee! Sometimes I call him that… Ha! You want to know how Jesus looks??? That's easy! Jesus is a tall man. He has kind of dark skin… Like a really dark kind of sun tan??? He usually wears a nice white robe that is soft like my Jimmy Bear Teddy.

He has brown eyes, the most amazing eyes you've ever seen. When you look into them, you get lost in there, right inside, and you never ever want to look away. You just want to live there in that place of warmth and perfect peace forever. His eyes are alive; they speak things without words. They tell me he loves me with no complication, no reasons. They tell me that he can't get enough of me. Just the way I'm feeling for him, that's how he loves, with his eyes alone.

His body is a wonder when you put it all together. He's kind of like Mr. Potato Head, I guess. All his parts fit together with something special, and in the end it creates something greater than great… much greater than Mr. Potato Head, in fact. Although I like that guy, he's funny.

His smile is… Well, I don't have words. It welcomes you to smile along with him. 'Cause even in the worst of painful times, he smiles gently at me and I have to smile back 'cause I know he ALWAYS loves me… Even if I've been bad.

His hands are both strong and gentle. It's crazy, 'cause you know he is God, but he touches you and sends warmth through you, right through your body down to your toes. Really, Bradley, you can feel warmer in your heart. Yet you know he is so, so strong too. One time when little Jacqueline [another dissociated part] was so hurt from the men who hurt her in the hospital… She was sad and crying and physically hurting. Jesus scooped her up and held her so softly in his strong arms. He stroked her hair, which was wet with tears and ran the back of his hand over and over her hot cheeks. Then when she was asleep, he gently placed her in the meeting chair and I saw a look of pain and rage and torment and anger on his face. He made his gentle hands into the strongest of fists. I couldn't believe this was my Jesus, that he was the same Jesus, because he looked so big and powerful. It kind of made me scared, but I liked it, too. It made me want to cheer for him because I knew he wasn't mad at Jacqueline. He was so tormented and angry at the man who would hurt one of his little ladies. She was only six years old. So, sorry I'm blabbering too long, but Jesus can be strong and mighty too.

Sitting on Jesus' lap is the best thing ever. When he holds out his hands, I HAVE to run to him, run so fast because he is waiting for me… Only me. Then he catches me and swings me up into the air. We play a lot, him and I, because I don't always like to sit still.

BUT THE BEST THING, my favorite thing… Is his hair!!! His hair is long and wavy and it feels like baby bunnies!!! When I cuddle with him, I sit and touch his hair. I run it through my fingers over and over. It helps put me to sleep. So, if you are ever having trouble sleeping, do that. It really, really helps. On special days he lets me play with his hair, and me and "J" [a third part] put it in ponytails. I think I told you that, but it's really, really true. Jesus with ponytails, isn't that funny?? Just think of it…

My favorite time ever is when Jesus talks to me. And he always talks to me. His voice is calm and gentle, yet when he means business... He means business. Sometimes I don't do what I'm told, and he does funny eyebrows. Remember? And sometimes he has to sit me down and tell me what I did wrong.

But something about Jesus that is different: he never raises his voice with me. He never makes me feel stupid or silly or bad. He just tells me that it isn't good for me or someone else. Or sometimes he says that Jesus just knows best and to trust him. That's a hard one sometimes.

And he loves when people do that… they let him take their lives. I struggle with that sometimes… well, a lot of the time, but Jesus doesn't make me feel bad… he just loves me. All the time… through everything… he just loves me is all. You know, other people tell me they love me and I sort of believe them… but with Jesus… you know it!!! And I love him, too, so, so much.

The greatest part is that I am learning that Jesus is big enough to love others that much, too. It isn't just for me. I used to be jealous when Jesus went to someone else inside… the other little girls (who are now my friends!). But now I am starting to see that Jesus can love others, too, everyone really. I'm still watching him closely, and I don't let him get too far away from me, but I think I am starting to be okay with it. I guess I am starting to want everyone to feel how special he is. It really shouldn't be just for me, should it? Anyway, I don't think I can stop Jesus from loving everyone. It's just what he does. I'm trying to learn how to do that, too. I like talking to you about Jesus, Bradley. He is everything to me. And to you, right??

I hope you liked what I told you about what Jesus is like to me. I'm not a very good book person, so you can change my words. You talk nicer than me.

It's hard to talk about Jesus, there's too much to say. And sometimes I don't use words 'cause they don't work. I just look in his eyes, and he talks to me without words. And I listen and watch, and I love him more and more. He is in my heart forever.

• • • • • •

Jesus said to pass on that some people aren't really "seeing" other people the way Jesus sees them. When we look at each other, are we really looking through Jesus' eyes? What are we really seeing? Are we letting the "world" in where we should be letting Jesus in?

The same goes for the way we see ourselves. Are we looking at ourselves and seeing what Jesus sees? Are we caring too much about what others think or see? When we look around, do we see "hearts" or just people? When Jesus looks at us, he sees our hearts, the way he intended us to be.

How are our eyes? How are we seeing?

Wow, Jesus just said, "It's time to lift the veil." Does that mean anything to you? I asked him what the veil was. He said the veil is different for everyone. We can have different veils at different times in our lives. The veil for me right now is self-hatred. What I think of myself and how I see myself clouds the truth, clouds my real self.

That was hard for me to share with someone. I'm trying to work on that, but it is hard. Nobody has ever seen me as good, but now some of them do. Like you, Bradley. You said

you see a miracle when you see me. That meant a lot to me.
I hope you know that. Do you know what your veil is right
now?

· · · · · ·

When I am with Jesus… I like me! When I am with Jesus, I
can feel how he sees me… I see it, too. When I move from
him, it's harder. I feel safe with him. I feel accepted. I feel
like I'm the most special girl in the whole world. And I want
others to feel that, too. All of the little girls inside, the teenagers too, I want it for everyone!!!

To Bradley
Love Eve

me and Jezuz having Tim Hortonz together.
It iz Mocha and not coffee for me.

Part 2

Being Jesus
to the Least Of These

Christs to One Another
Martin Luther[1]

Good things flow from Christ and are flowing into us. He has assumed us and acted for us as if he had been what we are. These good things flow from us onto those who have need of them so that we should lay before God our faith and righteousness that they may cover and intercede for the sins of our neighbor which we take on ourselves, and so labor and serve them as if they were our very own.

Surely, we are named after Christ, not because he is absent from us, but because he dwells within us; that is, because we believe in him and are *Christs to one another* and do to our neighbor as Christ does to us.

• • • • • •

The man who God has taken to Himself, sentenced and awakened to a new life, this is Jesus Christ. In Him, it is all mankind. It is ourselves.

Dietrich Bonhoeffer

---

[1] Martin Luther, *Luther's Works,* ed. Harold J. Grimm, vol. 31 (Philadelphia, PA: Fortress Press, 1957) 371, 368. Cited in Miroslav Volf, *Free of Charge: Giving and Forgiving in a Culture Stripped of Grace* (Grand Rapids, MI: Zondervan, 2006) 50-51.

7

"Did you come here to play Jesus?"

By Brad Jersak

"Did you come here to play Jesus? I did."
Bono

They spent some time in Jericho. As Jesus was leaving town, trailed by his disciples and a parade of people, a blind beggar by the name of Bartimaeus, son of Timaeus, was sitting alongside the road. When he heard that Jesus the Nazarene was passing by, he began to cry out, "Son of David, Jesus! Mercy, have mercy on me!" Many tried to hush him up, but he yelled all the louder, "Son of David! Mercy, have mercy on me!" Jesus stopped in his tracks. "Call him over." They called him. "It's your lucky day! Get up! He's calling you to come!" Throwing off his coat, he was on his feet at once and came to Jesus. Jesus said, "What can I do for you?" The blind man said, "Rabbi, I want to see." "On your way," said

Jesus. "Your faith has saved and healed you." In that very instant he recovered his sight and followed Jesus down the road. (Mark 10:46–52 MSG)

THE ATMOSPHERE in the arena was thick with anticipation—it literally felt humid. My friend Mike Stewart, who also happens to be a priest, and I were waiting for the concert to start. U2's *Vertigo* tour had rolled into Vancouver, and we were ready to join the throngs in welcoming the band. I didn't like our seats, but I thought that instead of grumbling about it, I would take a look for Jesus in the room. With the eyes of faith, I sensed that he might be settling into some "nosebleed seats" high in the balcony, ready with joy for the worship he would receive that night. I also sensed him speaking to my heart: "Watch Bono. At some point tonight, he and I will be interchangeable." I raised my eyebrows at this. Was my love of the band's frontman and his message distorting what I heard? Nevertheless, I felt such a strong presence of God in the place that I turned to Mike and said, "There's so much power in the room that if Bono says, 'Be healed,' I'll bet ten people would get healed. You watch!"

As the concert proceeded, Mike and I sang along at the top of our lungs. So many of the songs were direct prayers and modern Psalms. One song sorely missing from the set list that night was *Yahweh,*[1] in which Bono offers himself in service to God. In

---

[1] *Yahweh,* words and music by U2. From "How to Dismantle an Atomic Bomb," © 2004 Universal International Music BV.

twenty-first century metaphors, the lyrics echo the old hymn of consecration, *Take My Life and Let It Be.*[2]

In this updated version, Bono offers God his shoes, his shirt, and his soul, recognizing that grace must do a work to fit him and cleanse him for service. He gives God his hands, prone as they are to clenching into fists. He dedicates his mouth—"*so quick to criticize*"—and pleads for the kiss that will fill his mouth with good news. He finishes with a plea:

What no man can own, no man can take
Take this heart, take this heart,
Take this heart, and make it break.

He has and he will do all of these things, Bono. It's not just messiah complex or megalomania. God really has called us to "be Jesus" to others. To be his hands, his heart, his voice in this world. In fact, that night I actually saw it happen...

As the concert continued, I noticed a commotion down front. Someone had pushed a woman in a wheelchair through the mob toward the stage. She held up a large poster and kept waving it toward the stage. I was able to borrow some opera glasses from a fan behind me and had a good angle from which to read the sign. The large block letters said, "If I ditch this wheelchair, will you dance with me?"

Bono took note, stopped mid-stride, and spoke: "It pays

---

[2] Frances R. Havergal, February 1874. See page 245 for the full text.

to advertise." Then he extended his hand. The crowd actually picked up the woman and passed her from the chair over their heads to the stage. Bono pulled her up and they stood dancing for a brief time. It seemed awkward, she was wobbly, but she was dancing. Her jacket, which had been tied to her waist, fell to the floor and Bono stooped to pick it up and re-tie it. Then she stepped down off the stage, and Bono seemed to beckon the friend who had brought her. She was also passed up to the stage and danced for a bit.

> # IF I DITCH THIS WHEELCHAIR, WILL YOU DANCE WITH ME?

Mike and I looked at each other, amazed. My first thought was, *Is this for real?* Then, *This can't be a scam—her dance is far too awkward. And even if... What faith for Bono to reach out his hand!* Then I laughed, *If this is for real, how is Bono going to deal with the stigma of becoming a faith-healer?*

As always, the band left that night to the sound of the whole stadium singing acapella from Psalm 40—David's messianic prayer—in heartful unison. The original psalm reads this way in verse 1-3 of the New International Version:

I waited patiently for the LORD;
he turned to me and heard my cry.
He lifted me out of the slimy pit,
out of the mud and mire;
he set my feet on a rock
and gave me a firm place to stand.
He put a new song in my mouth,
a hymn of praise to our God.
Many will see and fear
and put their trust in the LORD.

Then all together, the crowd sang U2's refrain,

And I will sing, sing a new song.
I will sing, sing a new song.

Turning to Mike, I asked, "How do they do that? Upwards of twenty thousand people come together, most of whom would be horrified at the thought of entering a church. And these guys have us all singing with the angels."

Mike replied, "This is their gift. They can plant a prayer in our hearts—in *anyone's heart.*"

• • • • • •

I've been an eyewitness to enough medically verified healing miracles *and* silly shams that I'm neither unbelieving nor gullible. Nor am I obsessed with proving matters of faith, but still...

Hoping for verification, I tracked down my friend Pam, who confirmed that she saw the woman being wheeled in before the show from the parking lot. She appeared truly chair-bound. Later, Simon, one of Mike's congregants, shared that he was able to meet the woman on the floor after the concert. Sure enough, she was standing without the wheelchair, claiming "It's true. Nobody believes me, but this is real."

Truth or legend? To me, it seems the better question is, "Do I have the capacity to believe that the Christ of the Gospels is the same yesterday, today, and forever? Does he continue to stop midstream, take note of the least, and stretch out his hand to heal? Could he do it through Bono? Would he? Could he do it through me? Would he do it through you?"

This I know, *"He came to play Jesus...",* and so he did.

8

St. Francis the Healer[1]

THE TRUE DISCIPLE of Christ, St. Francis, as long as he lived in this miserable life, endeavoured with all his might to follow the example of Christ the perfect Master; whence it happened often, through the operation of grace, that he healed the soul at the same time as the body, as we read of Jesus Christ himself; and not only did he willingly serve the lepers himself, but he willed that all the brethren of his Order, both when they were travelling about the world and when they were halting on their way, should serve the lepers for the love of Christ, who for our sake was willing to be treated as a leper.

---

[1] Anonymous, "How St. Francis healed miraculously a leper both in his body and in his soul, and what the soul said to him on going up to heaven," *The Fioretti of St. Francis* (accessed 25 Jan. 2006) available from http://www.paxetbonum.net.

It happened once, that in a convent near the one in which St. Francis then resided there was a hospital for leprosy and other infirmities, served by the brethren; and one of the patients was a leper so impatient, so insupportable, and so insolent, that many believed of a certainty that he was possessed of the devil (as indeed he was) for he ill-treated with blows and words all those who served him; and, what was worse, he blasphemed so dreadfully our Blessed Lord and his most holy Mother the Blessed Virgin Mary, that none was found who could or would serve him. The brethren, indeed, to gain merit, endeavoured to accept with patience the injuries and violences committed against themselves, but their consciences would not allow them to submit to those addressed to Christ and to his Mother, wherefore they determined to abandon this leper, but this they would not do until they had signified their intention to St. Francis, according to the Rule.

On learning this, St. Francis, who was not far distant, himself visited this perverse leper, and said to him: "May God give thee peace, my beloved brother!"

To this the leper answered: "What peace can I look for from God, who has taken from me peace and every other blessing, and made me a putrid and disgusting object?"

St. Francis answered: "My son, be patient; for the infirmities of the body are given by God in this world for the salvation of the soul in the next; there is great merit in them when they are patiently endured."

The sick man answered: "How can I bear patiently the pain which afflicts me night and day? For not only am I greatly afflicted by my infirmity, but the friars thou hast sent to serve me make it even worse, for they do not serve me as they ought."

Then St. Francis, knowing through divine revelation that the leper was possessed by the malignant spirit, began to pray, interceding most earnestly for him. Having finished his prayer, he returned to the leper and said to him: "My son, I myself will serve thee, seeing thou art not satisfied with the others."

"Willingly," answered the leper; "but what canst thou do more than they have done?"

"Whatsoever thou wishest I will do for thee," answered St. Francis.

"I will then," said he, "that thou wash me all over; for I am so disgusting that I cannot bear myself."

Then St. Francis heated some water, putting therein many odoriferous herbs; he then undressed him, and began to wash him with his own hands, whilst another brother threw the water upon him, and, by a divine miracle, wherever St. Francis touched him with his holy hands the leprosy disappeared, and his flesh was perfectly healed also. On this the leper, seeing his leprosy beginning to vanish, felt great sorrow and repentance for his sins, and began to weep bitterly. While his body was being purified externally of the leprosy through the cleansing of the water, so his soul internally was purified from sin by the washing of tears and repentance; and feeling himself completely healed both in his body and his soul, he humbly confessed his sins, crying out in a loud voice, with many tears: "Unhappy me! I am worthy of hell for the wickedness of my conduct to the brethren, and the impatience and blasphemy I have uttered against the Lord";

and for fifteen days he ceased not to weep bitterly for his sins, imploring the Lord to have mercy on him, and then made a general confession to a priest.

St. Francis, perceiving this evident miracle which the Lord had enabled him to work, returned thanks to God, and set out for a distant country; for out of humility he wished to avoid all glory, and in all his actions he sought only the glory of God and not his own. It pleased God that the leper, who had been healed both in his body and in his soul, after having done penance for fifteen days, should fall ill of another infirmity; and having received the sacraments of the Church, he died a most holy death.

His soul on its way to heaven appeared in the air to St. Francis, who was praying in a forest, and said to him: "Dost thou know me?"

"Who art thou?" Asked the saint.

Said he: "I am that leper whom our Blessed Lord healed through thy merits, and today I am going to life eternal, for which I return thanks to God and to thee. Blessed by thy soul and thy body, blessed by thy holy words and works, for through thee many souls are saved in the world; and know that there is not a single day in which the angels and other saints do not return thanks to God for the holy fruits of thy preaching and that of thy Order in various parts of the world. Be comforted, then, and thank the Lord, and may his blessing rest on thee." Having said these words, he went up to heaven, leaving St. Francis much consoled.

9

Angel Gown

By Irene Jersak

I GREW UP ON A FARM about ten miles from Ashern, Manitoba, Canada. I was the eighth of nine children. Though my parents worked very hard, we didn't have much, and winters could be especially hard.

In December when I was about six years old, my little country schoolhouse put on a Christmas concert, and the teacher said that I was to be one of the angels. I would have been very excited about this, but the teacher said that for my costume, I would need a nightgown that would reach all the way to my feet. I felt very bad, because I had nothing of the sort, and I knew I mustn't burden my parents by asking for one. I couldn't bring myself to tell anyone, so I just worried myself sick. Days and rehearsals passed, and I still saw no solution in sight.

A day or two before the concert, my father hitched up his caboose to the horses and headed off to town to do errands. When he returned, he had a surprise for the family. He had checked in at the post office, where he found an unexpected parcel. There was a clothing gift for each child, perfectly matched to their size, age, and gender. When it came to me, out came a beautiful white flannelette nightgown! It was like new, with three little pearls buttoned down from the Peter Pan collar, a gathered yoke in front and back with gathers descending from there. It was full length, right to my feet, with frills all around the bottoms and the cuffs.

I stood there in disbelief. Then I tried it on. It was perfect! I really felt like a beautiful angel. Wearing it to the concert, I felt like a little princess! But where had it come from? Who could have known?

• • • • • •

Six months earlier, during the summer, a grey station wagon had pulled onto the yard. Two Anglican nuns in grey dresses had come to pay us a visit, and my mother invited them to stay for a meal. While the ladies ate with us, they silently observed each of the children, assessing our needs and quietly calculating our ages and sizes. After dinner, they waved goodbye and off they went. Perhaps I was not the only angel in this story...

10

Jenni Plays Jesus

By Jenni Kornell

Is not this the kind of fasting I have chosen: to loose the chains of injustice and untie the cords of the yoke, to set the oppressed free and break every yoke?

Isaiah 58:6

IT'S NOT LIKE I PLANNED THIS. I did not wake up one morning and decide that today I would take on the greatest evil I could ever imagine. For the most part, it was "just" another day, but then something happened that changed my life by showing me what I was called to do.

It was a remarkably warm evening in the Southeast Asian city in which I was living. I had my lesson planning books and was going to sit in the air-conditioned comfort of Starbucks to plan for the English classes I was teaching. I parked my little motorcycle at the side of the road and began to walk down the busy street towards the coffee shop. I was very familiar with the road and had gotten to know many of the people that worked along its busy sidewalks. They would often smile and say hello to me, and this evening was no exception.

I paused for a moment to check the traffic before venturing out across the street. As I paused, I noticed an old man with a young girl. I had seen this kind of scene many times before, a child selling roses to the foreigners who pitied them. I had purchased flowers on many occasions from these same children. But this child had no flowers or anything else to sell that I could see.

I crossed the street, my eyes focused on this unnatural exchange. I was close enough to see the old man give this young girl money, about $20. Then he took her little hand and led her down the street. I was close enough to hear him speak to her in thickly accented English, close enough to smell the smoke from his cigarette. As they walked away from the city centre, for some reason I decided to follow them. I had no idea what I was going to do, but I followed them.

When they reached a street where cars could park, he let her hand go as he reached into his pocket. At that moment, I grabbed the little girl, tossed her over my shoulders, and ran down the street back to the safety of the bright lights and familiar people. It must have looked rather comical to anyone watching, but let me assure you, I was terrified, and I had no idea what I was going to do next.

I saw the owner of a shop that I had been to many times and ran into his store. I left the little girl with him then went back out front to face a VERY ANGRY European man. He yelled and screamed and said that he was a friend of the child's mother, told me that I was making a big mistake, and threatened me. I just stood there and took it, then reached slowly into my pocket and took out my camera phone. I snapped his picture and told him, "I'm sending this to your embassy!" This made him back off, but while he walked away, he continued to mutter to himself and to the small crowd of people that had gathered to watch the confrontation. Most of the crowd did not speak English, so it was easy to get them to dissipate. I am not sure what they thought they had just witnessed, but I am certain they thought it was rather normal for white people to behave in such strange ways.

At that point, I looked down and saw my new young friend and realized I had no plan. I had no idea what I, a single young woman teaching English in Southeast Asia, was going to do with a six-year-old.

I checked my watch. It was about eight o'clock. I chatted with the girl for a few minutes and realized she needed a place to stay for the night. While I knew it was not going to be a long-term solution, I decided to let her stay at my house and then work out a better plan in the morning. As we were preparing to leave on my motorcycle, she pulled on my sleeve. I stopped to listen, and she told me she had a little sister. We got off the motorcycle and she took me down a nearby alley. There she was, standing in front of a "massage parlour," a tiny, four-year-old girl, eyes drooping from being so tired and clothes dirty from sitting in the street all day. What choice did I have? She looked so vulnerable, and as I spoke to her, she just came and wrapped her little arms around me and let me carry her back down the street to my motorcycle.

It was now about nine at night and I had two children with me that I had no idea what to do with. Once again, as we prepared to leave the downtown area, I felt a tug on my sleeve. Sure enough, there was another sister that needed to come with us.

My two new friends led me to a run-down house that I learned later was a rather well known brothel. I walked in and asked for the girl, and she came out front with me to talk to her little sisters. The sight of those three girls talking to one another and all so desperate and vulnerable made me feel protective. I am sure this is how parents feel about their own children. I could not imagine how I could walk away from them now. It was as though an unseen bond had developed between us. It all happened so quickly, but somehow I felt they were now my responsibility.

As the eldest sister, a waif-like girl of fourteen, asked me if it would be okay if she brought her son with us, I honestly felt calm and relaxed and even laughed as I told her that her son was more than welcome.

So there we were, a four-year-old, a six-year-old, a fourteen-year-old, a four-month-old, and a twenty-nine-year-old white woman. None of us had any idea of what had just happened or the changes that this was going to bring about in our lives, but we proceeded forward anyway.

Over the next few days, the two little girls were placed in a home for children that met all of their needs, they were able to go to school, play with kids their own age, and get appropriate counseling. The fourteen-year-old and her son stayed with me. She began learning how to read and write and gained some valuable skills, such as sewing and gardening. She also received the counseling she needed to become a good mother and provider for her son.

Over the next few months my reason for being in Southeast Asia had changed. Eventually, I quit my job and found a location that would be able to house more than just the few of us. A friend of mine from an NGO (non-governmental organization) called Hope for the Nations took on this project and provided invaluable support for obtaining finances and other resources. I found other organizations locally and regionally who were doing similar work and was able to learn from their experience and expertise. I also threw myself into language study so I would be able to communicate effectively with the children and young women that I was now meeting on a regular basis.

After I share this story, I am always asked two questions: "Weren't you scared?" and "What happened to all of those girls?" The two youngest girls are still in a children's home and are being well taken care of. The fourteen-year-old has gone back to the brothel, but she stays in contact with us. She wants to leave but knows that she will make more money at the brothel than doing anything else. Her son is in a village being cared for by his grandmother. It is not ideal; it is not even close, but it is the type of reality that frontline aid workers deal with daily.

As for the second question, yes, I was scared. I was terrified, actually, but not for me. I was frightened for what would happen to these girls had I not intervened. In that moment, I forgot all about the things that are important to me and caught a glimpse of God's heart for these girls. In that moment, I learned that he is a God that requires us to respond to the needs around us, a God that would not let harm happen to these girls for one more night, a God that demanded my action. To walk away was not an option for me. It is not an option for anyone.

11

Mercy

By Darla Faulkner

The following story is a true account of one of my experiences in working with "the least of these" in Africa. To protect the identity of the child in this story, the name of the organization and the country in which I worked has been withheld.

I MOVED TO AFRICA in 2002 to work as the director of a home for children who were affected by HIV/AIDS. During my time there, I experienced many challenges and heartaches as I witnessed the devastation that the HIV/AIDS pandemic is wreaking on that continent. Working in the midst of so much grief and human suffering on a daily basis was difficult. I would be painting a false picture for you if I said otherwise. The anger, frustration, and despair that I felt each time I held a dying child in my arms will not be soon forgotten. Yet in the midst of this heartache were many moments of joy, moments when I realized that a child had beaten the odds and his or her health and dignity had been restored. Mercy was one of these children. Here is her story…

Mercy grew up in a shanty compound without electricity or running water and often went days without food. Her parents did not have enough money to send her to school, so Mercy spent most of her days begging in the local market.

When Mercy was only five years old, she lost both of her parents to AIDS. If the pain and suffering from poverty, malnutrition, and losing her parents were not difficult enough, Mercy was shunned by her community and taken in by an abusive relative. Mercy endured four long years of physical and sexual abuse at the hands of her relative before she was rescued.

When our organization heard of Mercy's plight, there was not a shadow of doubt in anyone's mind—we had to step in. After a visit to the police station and social welfare, Mercy was removed from her painful environment and brought into our children's home; where she was provided with the appropriate medical attention and counselling. Like most of the children who had come into our home, Mercy was malnourished, underdeveloped, and diagnosed with several sexually transmitted diseases. Although I had heard this diagnosis several times before, I had never been able to stomach it. It sickened me to know that Mercy had suffered such horrific abuse. Once again, I was filled with many mixed emotions. I was irate and frustrated that Mercy's relative never spent a day behind bars. I was angered by every injustice that Mercy had experienced in her short life. And once again, I was broken.

After six months of a well-balanced diet, counseling, proper medical attention, and schooling, Mercy was well on her way to having her health and dignity restored.

One year after Mercy was registered into our children's home, we were asked to host a luncheon for the Second Lady of the country (the Vice President's wife), the mayor of the city, and the local press. A week before the luncheon was to take place, Mercy asked if I would allow her to write a play for our esteemed guest and then let her and the other children perform it. When I asked her what the play would be about, she quickly informed me that she wanted it to be a surprise, not just for the Second Lady and the other guests, but for me as well. I must admit that I was extremely hesitant to give Mercy permission to put on a play for our nation's leaders without previewing it first, but I reluctantly agreed.

On the day of the performance, Mercy and the other children were extremely excited. They had been practising all week and felt confident that their play would be great. I still remember how nervous I felt sitting next to the Second Lady and the mayor, before the play started. I was excited that the children had the opportunity to have the undivided attention of some of the nation's top leaders, and yet I was nervous about the content of the play. Did the children really understand who they were performing for?

As I watched the story line unfold, I was absolutely shocked. Mercy had written a play about a man who drank a lot of beer and cheated on his wife. The man had several children with his wife as well as with the other women. Eventually, the man contracted AIDS and ended up infecting his wife and the other women. The play ended with the man, his wife, and the other women dying, leaving their children orphaned.

When the closing scene was finished, Mercy stood in the centre of the stage and addressed the audience boldly: "You adults think you can do whatever you want and it won't hurt your children, but you're wrong. That's what our parents thought, and now they're dead. They died of AIDS, and one day most of us will die, because they gave it to us, too. Grow up! There are not enough children's homes in our country to take care of your children after you're dead! Thank you for coming to our show."

The whole audience sat in complete silence, tears streaming down our faces, as the children bowed and laughed and ran off stage. After I got over the initial shock of watching a ten-year-old girl rebuke the nation's leaders, the content of the play and the rebuke began to sink in. Mercy was bold enough to share her story, unapologetically, with the nation. She used the pain and suffering of her past to influence the future of her people. I have never felt this proud of anyone before, nor have I ever felt so humbled.

Knowing Mercy has changed my life forever. Her story has challenged me to turn the pain and suffering of my past into a powerful tool to influence the future. She has taught me the real importance of standing up for what I believe and, more importantly, not to apologize for who I am and where I come from.

After I share this story, I am often confronted with two

questions: What about the millions of other children out there? We were only able to have thirty-five children in our children's home at any given time. Considering the statistics, this isn't even a drop in the bucket, so why bother?

The answer to these questions is this: The HIV/AIDS pandemic is sweeping across the African continent at an alarming rate and is affecting millions of innocent children just like Mercy. As adult mortality rates increase and the number of orphans continues to grow, the world faces the formidable challenge of clothing the naked, feeding the hungry, and taking care of the sick. Although the economic and social impact of this pandemic is overwhelming, meeting the needs of the "least of these" is possible. It becomes possible when we break down the overwhelming statistics and put names, faces, and stories to the numbers. We should bother because each person, each child, is an individual who has been created in the image of God, each bearing talents, abilities and personalities that are as unique as yours or mine. Making a difference is possible when we *see and be Jesus* to the least of these. If Mercy was the only child I was able to help, it was worth it. After all, her story challenged a nation. Who knows what might result?

Part 3

Meeting Jesus
through the Least Of These

12

Trading My Sorrows

By Brad Jersak

A S IF THE CANOPY is not already lively enough, I suppose those who were there shall never forget the antics of Meghan, an autistic girl who was perhaps eight years old at the time.

The Canopy is a fresh, arts-friendly church in Edmonton, Alberta, Canada. I was the guest speaker for a weekend "Listening Prayer" conference. On Sunday morning, I was preparing to speak on "Seeing Jesus in Others" when Meghan became the living illustration.

As we spent some time singing worship songs, Meghan marched spontaneously to the front and began dancing before the band. She used the full width of the stage to twirl ballerina-like from left to right. Then she performed a very exuberant and formal goose-step back to the left. This was followed by an over-the-top aggressive headbanger kind of dance, flinging her locks round and round like a living windmill. She punctuated this by throwing herself to her knees and treating us to an air guitar solo. With plenty of energy left, she crossed the stage yet again with another dance step. She seemed to be completely oblivious to the crowd, entirely in her own secret world. I'm not quite sure the congregation knew what to do with this demonstration of wanton freedom. For my part, I was totally captivated.

One thing I've learned about autism is that sometimes you can enter that secret world by mimicking the child (or adult as the case may be), so that is what I proceeded to do. What a sight as suddenly the guest teacher and the little girl repeated the odd *anti*-choreography together—now twirling, now marching, now thrashing. Scoff, but as King David once said having danced with absolute abandon, "I will become even more undignified than this!" (2 Sam. 6:21-22)

Sure enough, little Meghan connected. She made that elusive eye-contact with me, and we were locked in. Unfortunately, it wasn't long before this out-of-shape preacher was huffing and puffing and holding his pounding chest. I took a breather, doubled over as the music continued. At that point, she walked up to me, grabbed my head, and pulled it close enough that our foreheads were touching. Then looking me in the eye, she proclaimed enthusiastically, "You've been to Scotland." And then she "went off" as they say, "Hi Scot! Scot-Man! Scot, Scot, Scot. You've been to Scotland."

I was stunned. What Meghan did not and could not have known was that I had just returned from Scotland. So recently, in fact, that I was still in the final stages of recovery from a bout of jet lag. Now she had my attention! But of course, off she returned to her private world of dance, leaving me to sort out the significance of the information that she seemingly extracted from my weary head.

She danced a while more then came skipping back to me, this time miming some very disturbing sign language in rhythm with the music. She would point directly at me with her index finger. Then she would slowly draw the index finger across her throat in a dramatic slitting action, followed again by the pointing finger. It certainly felt like she was predicting my demise, and the accuracy of her first revelation made me hesitant to dismiss her too quickly. (I've learned that the hard way over the years.)

Meghan's grandmother, who had brought her to church that morning, saw what was happening and scurried forward to "rescue me."

"Let me take her away. She's autistic."

"Don't you dare!" I shouted to her over the music. "This means something. I need to know what she's trying to say."

Just then, the Lord spoke to my heart in a tone that sounded like, "How dull are you? Don't you get it?" (Matthew 17:17) What he actually said was, "You're singing it!"

He was right. I didn't get it. "What do you mean?" I asked. He said it again, "You're singing it." Finally, I had my "Aha!"

moment. As Meghan continued to gesture, I awoke to the fact that I was singing along without thinking about the lyrics:

I'm trading my sorrows
I'm trading my shame
I'm laying them down for the joy of the Lord

I'm trading my sickness
I'm trading my pain
I'm laying them down for the joy of the Lord

As I watched Meghan continue, I could see that she was pointing at the words "sorrow" and "shame" and "sickness" and "pain" and then cursing them with the cutting motion. Whether she was tuned into this or merely God's simple vessel, I could see Jesus in her, cursing weariness, jet lag, and sickness in my body. Somehow he gave me the capacity to receive this gift, such that I could truthfully feel them being laid down in exchange for joy, health, and refreshment. Through my new friend Meghan, Christ restored my body, soul, and spirit in a matter of minutes.

Imagine my delight to be able to point to that little girl and bring the good news to her church—a church that gives space for disabled children to dance before the Lord. As Jesus said,

Therefore whoever humbles himself as this little child is the greatest in the kingdom of heaven. Whoever receives one little child like this in My name receives Me. (Matthew 18: 4–5 NKJV)

13

Keepers of the Book

By Brad Jersak

Eddie, Tom, and Phil attend Fresh Wind Christian Fellowship. Each has a unique pastoral gift. Though it seems that none of them can read, they are all lovers of the Scriptures. When you look in their faces, some might see Down's Syndrome or autism. But we see Jesus.

Pastor Eddie

EDDIE IS A PASTOR in our church. You'll see him sitting faithfully in the aisle seat, second row on the right, every Sunday morning. He's quite recognizable with his Tai Chi-like dance moves and the leather-bound Bible under his arm. He loves to rise spontaneously and give the closing benediction, whether or not the preacher thinks the sermon is finished.

The fact that he has Down's Syndrome has long been a non-issue to us, for his reputation as a shepherd has washed that label away. I only mention it here as an advocate for those like Eddie whose deep wisdom and spirituality are too often underestimated—such a loss to the Body of Christ.

Eddie has a deep love for the Scriptures. He doesn't necessarily read, but I'm told that he pours over the pages, meticulously underlining verse after verse for hours on end. It's as if his spirit, which is and always has been fully functional, is absorbing the Spirit of "the Book." For this reason, we take it very seriously when he brings us his open Bible and points to the text, indicating that we should read it to the congregation. These readings have proven to be a consistent blessing to each of us, and especially to me personally.

"Eddie"

One Sunday, I was scheduled to preach on "God's Heart for the Poor" but was struggling with whether or not I was qualified. I had just purchased my first home and entered the rather daunting new world of mortgages. Had I compromised myself and lost the right to speak to the poor at all? What happened to being a "sojourner?" I asked the Lord, "How can I preach on this? I'm sure that you led us into this home, and I'm sure of your concern for the poor, but what right have I to share this message?" No answer seemed to be forthcoming, so I proceeded to the church, quite open to handing off the homily to someone else.

As we entered a time of worship, I was still wrestling with God and scheming about who I could ask to step in for me. Thankfully, I was standing in the first row, right in front of Eddie. As I gave the Lord his last chance to speak to me before I pulled the plug, I felt a tap on my shoulder. Eddie had his Bible open and was pointing to a specific paragraph on the page.

I asked, "Do you have a verse for me?" He gave a big nod and said an emphatic "YES." I took the Bible and read:

This is the Message from GOD-of-the-Angel-Armies, Israel's God, to all the exiles I've taken from Jerusalem to Babylon: "Build houses and make yourselves at home. Put in gardens and eat what grows in that country. Marry and have children. Encourage your children to marry and have children so that you'll thrive in that country and not waste away. Make yourselves at home there and work for the country's welfare. Pray for Babylon's well-being. If things go well for Babylon, things will go well for you." (Jeremiah 29:4–7)

God's message came through loud and clear. *Yes, you are*

first and foremost a citizen of heaven and, as such, an exile living in Canada. But go ahead and settle down, buy a house, raise your family. Just be sure to be a blessing to the nation where I've put you, especially remembering to bless the poor with the blessings you have received.

I looked up at Eddie's satisfied grin. He knew somehow that he had hit the bull's-eye of my heart. The look on his face said, "See?" And the twinkle in his eye was that of Jesus.

Pastor Tom

So far, Fresh Wind is a church that has avoided the traps inherent in titles. For years we were wary of calling anyone

"Tom"

"pastor" because of the stereotypes and misrepresentations that accompany such a label. However, in Tom's case, we felt the Lord give us a green light. When I asked why it was safe to call him a pastor, the answer I received was, "Tom's the one person in the church who won't get any 'bright ideas' when you call him that."

Touché.

Tom attends my home group. When he's not hamming it up, he says powerful prayers that include sign language, Tom's own language, lyrics from "Jesus loves me," and some Benedictine style "amens" when he concludes. But he is also one of the "Keepers of the Book," regularly pulling out a real zinger from the Bible on just the right occasion.

In the final hour leading up to America's announcement of their second invasion of Iraq, our group was meeting for prayer. We asked Jesus what to pray for and then listened. Attendees began to speak up: "Pray for Iraq." "Pray for the children of Iraq." "Pray for President Bush." "Pray for wisdom for Mr. Bush."

There was a period of silence as I thought about what real wisdom might look and sound like in the Iraq crisis. At precisely that moment, Tom stood up and opened his Bible, indicating that someone should read a passage he had found. Charles Littledale, our fearless leader, took the Bible and read:

> Who is a wise man and endued with knowledge among you? Let him shew out of a good conversation his works with meekness of wisdom. But if ye have bitter envying and strife in your hearts, glory not, and lie not against the truth. This wisdom descendeth not from above, but is earthly, sensual, devilish. For where envying and strife is, there is confusion and every evil work. But the wisdom that is from above is first pure, then peaceable, gentle, and easy to be intreated, full of mercy and good fruits, without partiality, and without hypocrisy. And the fruit of righteousness is sown in peace of them that make peace. (James 3:13–18 KJV)

I felt the impact of those words. I felt the intentions of the White House. And I felt the fear of the Lord. Tom had delivered the Word of the Lord—an indictment on all parties who reject the wisdom of heaven in favour of vengeance and violence. I don't understand all the complexities behind the wars we wage. But I know this: Both James and Tom consider them folly.

"Philled"

Last but not least of the "three amigos" is Phil. His skilled use of the "sword of the Spirit" has earned him the right to choose our regular weekly Bible reading at our home group. Whichever text he chooses becomes the topic of discussion. His pick is typically poignant... and always potent.

It's not uncommon for him to unknowingly find a Scripture that matches the theme of the songs we've sung that evening. When we did an entire set list involving mercy (theme song: "Mercy is Falling"), Phil had Charles read Psalm 123:2.

> Behold, as the eyes of servants look unto the hand of their masters, and as the eyes of a maiden unto the hand of her mistress; so our eyes wait upon the LORD our God, until that he have mercy upon us.

One night, Phil opened his Bible to Titus 3. Before I could take the Bible from him to read it, he closed it up. So I asked, "Aren't you going to give us a passage?" Again, he opened to Titus 3 (odd, seeing as he appeared to be flipping randomly through the pages). Then he closed the Bible again. Then, for a third time, he opened to Titus 3. The odds of this were extremely slim, but I passed it off as the luck of the book binding.

Meanwhile, Phil seemed troubled. Then Charles finally realized Phil was gazing lustfully at the BIG Bible across the room. Charles asked Phil if he wanted to use that Bible instead, to which Phil responded with a huge grin. Taking the Bible in hand, he flipped purposefully through many hundreds

"Phil"

of cigarette-paper-thin pages all the way to... Titus 3!

> To speak evil of no man, to be no brawlers, but gentle, shewing all meekness unto all men. For we ourselves also were sometimes foolish, disobedient, deceived, serving divers lusts and pleasures, living in malice and envy, hateful, and hating one another. But after that the kindness and love of God our Saviour toward man appeared, Not by works of righteousness which we have done, but according to his mercy he saved us, by the washing of regeneration, and renewing of the Holy Ghost; Which he shed on us abundantly through Jesus Christ our Saviour; That being justified by his grace, we should be made heirs according to the hope of eternal life. (Titus 3:2–7 KJV)

The passage definitely impacted us, if for no reason other than that God had led Phil to the passage four times in two different Bibles. We resolved to keep our eyes and ears open that week to see if we could discern its relevance to our situation.

The following evening, our worship leader (Karen), attended a home group in another church, where she recounted the story of Phil and his fixation with Titus 3. They spent the evening meditating on the passage, deciding again to stay alert for its potential meaning.

The leaders of the home group, Ian and Lorraine, carried the passage in their hearts until Sunday when they went to their church and heard a guest preacher speak on... You guessed it, Titus 3! After the service, the couple headed out to visit Lorraine's father, who had been institutionalized due to severe dementia. He had suffered with the affliction for several years and was now in sharp decline. He didn't recognize Lorraine or Ian, could no longer walk or talk (other than mumbling), and would sit in his chair staring blankly into space. Nevertheless, the couple still felt it was important to sit and talk with him regularly, to connect with him as family. On the way to the institution, they decided to tell Lorraine's dad the story of Phil and then read Titus 3.

Settling in, they opened the Bible and started reading. When they got to the phrase: "hateful, and hating one another," Lorraine's dad spoke! "That was me," he said, becoming fully lucid for the first time in years. Shocked, the couple continued to read. When they got to the phrase, "made heirs according to the hope of eternal life," her dad asserted, "That's what I want!" They prayed together, asking God to come and give Lorraine's dad the hope of eternal life in Jesus. He received this hope gladly... And then lapsed back into dementia! What happened? What was this marvelous chain of events from Phil to Lorraine's dad? This conspiracy of saving grace? Here was our conclusion: Lorraine's dad got *"Philled."*

Amen!

14

Kathy

By Brad Jersak

Kathy West leads a home group for Fresh Wind. She is especially blessed as a worship leader.

Human wisdom is so tiny, so impotent, next to the seeming absurdity of God. Human strength can't begin to compete with God's "weakness." Take a good look, friends, at who you were when you got called into this life. I don't see many of "the brightest and the best" among you, not many influential, not many from high-society families. Isn't it obvious that God deliberately chose men and women that the culture overlooks and exploits and abuses, chose these "nobodies" to expose the hollow pretensions of the "somebodies"?

1 Corinthians 1:25–28 MSG

K ATHY WEST IS A PILLAR who helped in the formation of our little faith family. We have often seen Jesus in her smile and heard him in her voice. Like Eddie, she might seem disabled to outsiders, but when she prays, "Come, Jesus," we experience her as a wonderful lightning rod of God's grace. Looks can be deceiving, for she is bound to a wheelchair, blind in one eye, and endures constant pain in what's left of her hips. But within her broken body you will find a lively girl with an enormous capacity for God's presence.

During a renewal service I attended one evening in the late 1990s, a space had been cleared at the front for the children and

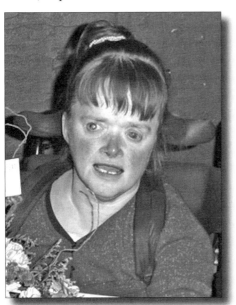

the childlike to dance and celebrate. Kathy showed up a little late, but rather than relegating her to the back of the room, her careworkers brought her right into the thick of the dance. I had just met her a few months earlier, but I already knew to keep an eye open for what God might be up to around this lively woman.

"Kathy"

Immediately, a little crowd of children formed a circle around Kathy, holding hands, singing praises, and dancing. This "ring around the Kathy" moment was a beautiful display of God's kingdom, and Kathy was enjoying it thoroughly. As worship continued, the children skipped away, and I had a chance to sidle up to her. I felt her hand in mine and thought I'd invite God to love me through her. I started to feel a little woozy, and a quiet inner voice spoke to my heart past the din of the band, "You'd better lay down, boy."

"Are you about to download something of Kathy's spiritual strength to me?" I asked.

To which the voice repeated, "You'd better lay down."

Occasionally, I'm actually smart enough to obey. So right there and then, I laid down on the floor beside Kathy's wheelchair, still holding her hand. Suddenly, what felt like a powerful jolt of electricity drove through my body. It felt like the time I grabbed the bare section of a 220-volt drill press wire. I caught my breath just in time for a second jolt. Then a third. It seemed to me that this was a power-of-God-thing, but it was so intense that I prayed, "God, I want everything you have for me. Help me not to beg you to stop." Four. Five. I was counting the jolts. Six. Seven. Kathy kept hanging on. Eight. Nine. The seizures must have looked ridiculous. Ten. Eleven. Twelve. Kathy let go, dropping my limp arm to the floor. She just sort of smirked, then carried on in worship.

"What was that about?" I asked God, hoping for some kind of an explanation. Nothing. What was the point of this cattle-prod exercise? For several days, I pondered it in my heart. I didn't feel any different. No real character change. No new gifts of the Spirit. Apart from the "Wow!" factor, the entire episode seemed pointless.

• • • • • •

A few days after this incident, my cousin Merilee called me from Calgary. She was couch-ridden with an ailment that manifested lupus-like symptoms. She felt like her body was falling apart and, in this case, she felt her back and shoulder "go out," her arm hanging limp without strength.

I had just read an article that weekend in a medical journal about lupus-like symptoms caused by repressed anger from work-related stress. (A coincidence?) I asked if this rang a bell. As it turned out, she had a run-in with a raging customer at work that day. To maintain an image of professionalism, she had suppressed her anger. But the moment the customer left, Merilee's body shut down. We prayed together over the phone, telling Jesus how she *really* felt and asking him to lift the anger and its effects from her body.

Within seconds, she starting yelping over the phone. *"Half my pain just disappeared!"* Being a man of enormous faith, I replied, "No way! You're lying!"

"I am not! I'm standing up, and I can move my arm!"

So we asked the Lord if there were any other instances of repressed anger that she needed to hand over to God. He showed her one involving a relative, where, for the sake of peace, she had also swallowed her ire. Again, God took it, and Merilee cried over the phone, "It's gone! The pain is all gone! I'm actually swinging my arm around like a windmill!" My unbelief got the best of me once more, but it was true. While Merilee continues to learn how to cope with health issues, this bout was over in a matter of minutes.

When I debriefed with God in prayer, I asked, "Why was Merilee healed so quickly and completely? That's not normal for me. Where did that power come from?"

He replied, "That came from me and from Kathy. You were just the "capacitor," (a temporary storage unit for power) storing my power until Merilee needed it." What could I say? I signed off not with a hearty "Amen" but with a humble "Oh." St. Paul said, "God has chosen the weak and foolish things to confound the [so-called] wise and strong" (cf. 1 Corinthians 1:27). That looks good on paper, but what if he really meant it? How might that look in this world that exalts competence and expertise? How might that look in the Church, which has been co-opted by the world system of hierarchical power?

Kathy West is my constant reminder that God's kingdom is much different than our kingdoms. It is the realm where those who exalt themselves are humbled, and the humble are exalted; where true greatness is achieved through servanthood; and where downward mobility is the name of the game.

15

"You need to think with your heart"

By Brad Jersak

And a little child shall lead them.

Isaiah 11:6

JESUS ONCE SAID,

Assuredly, I say to you, unless you are converted and become
as little children, you will by no means enter the kingdom
of heaven. Therefore whoever humbles himself as this little
child is the greatest in the kingdom of heaven. *Whoever
receives one little child like this in My name receives Me.*
(Matthew 18:3–5 NKJV)

What if Jesus meant these words? And if he did mean them,
how shall we respond? Much has been said on the importance of
childlike faith and welcoming children in Jesus' name, but I'm

less convinced that we've actually lived it. If we really believed Christ visits us and speaks to us through children, perhaps we'd be slower to dismiss them to the church basement when it's time to "get serious with God." Maybe we would take Jesus' admonition as a sincere invitation to hear him speak through these little ones. I'm excited to see this happening more and more across the Body of Christ.

While pastoring in Alberta, my friends Tim and Sara Warriner noted that most of the life and worship in their church was expressed through the children. The question was raised, "Then why do we send them downstairs while the adults sit on their hands in the nice room?" They chose to flip this arrangement, letting the children take over the sanctuary until the adults were ready to ascend to the place where they could be led into kingdom life. They took Jesus seriously, saying, "If we can't hear him in the children, will we hear him at all?"

The more we acknowledge this truth, the thinner the veil between our realm and the heavenly dimension becomes. I am reminded of two children in particular. In this chapter, you will meet Kezia and in the next, the remarkable "Cinder-Ella."

Kezia

Kezia is the daughter of my friend Mike, an Anglican priest. He and his wife Marianne have shown their daughter Kezia from a young age that they take seriously the presence of Jesus within her. The little things that come out of her mouth are treated as precious, thus nurturing her awareness of her friendship with

God. Here are some "Kezia-isms" from when she was four and five-years-old.

"Kezia"

One truth that Kezia teaches us is that Christ is with us always, not watching passively, but interacting with his children throughout the day. Mike says that sometimes Kezia will fall to the floor laughing and squirming, claiming that Jesus is tickling her. On other occasions, she'll begin to weep, testifying that Jesus is speaking to her, telling her that she is his princess and his little flower. Her tears come because, she says, "The things he says are so lovely. And sometimes he sings to me at night."

In fact, every night, Kezia goes to sleep with a picture of a little girl sleeping on Jesus' lap on heaven's throne (from my book, *Children, Can You Hear Me?*). She says, "Jesus said I can fall asleep on his lap any time I want to. That way I can get more 'Jesus-ness' in my heart."

Usually, she is able to locate Jesus in the room with the eyes of faith (e.g. "Jesus isn't here yet... Oh, here he comes!"). She will set up a cozy little nest on her bed where Jesus and her can talk. Her prayers may include giggling and saying, "Oh, Jesus!" as he says something to make her blush. How cute—but wait, don't underestimate her. Jesus said, "See that you do not look down on one of these little ones. For I tell you that their angels in heaven always see the face of my Father in heaven." (Matthew 18:10 NIV)

Sometimes her words can pack a real punch. One day as Mike was rebuking her for something at the table, four-year-old Kezia lifted her finger, and, staring him down, said in her little English accent, "When I'm naughty, Jesus isn't cross with me. Jesus says you must learn to think with your heart. Sometimes you are mean with your mouth. You must learn to think with your heart."

One morning, she ran into the kitchen, shouting, "Mummy, there's a man in your shower!" and then took off back down to the en suite where she saw him. Of course, Marianne was startled. Mike had already gone to work and there shouldn't have been any man in the house, much less the shower. We have enough home invasions in Vancouver that it put a scare in her. Before the panic could deepen, Kezia called back down the hall, "It's okay. It's just Jesus. He's painting red hearts on your shower walls!"

As it turns out, this was significant, because the night before, Mike had come home from church carrying an overload of burdens. He had taken a shower and, in that space, had a powerful visitation of grace whereby God gave him a spiritual shower. Kezia was seeing the residual effects of that encounter.

Kezia represents a growing number of children who know, like little Lucy from *The Chronicles of Narnia,* that Aslan (God) is on the move. We dare not ignore their testimony.

16

Cinder-Ella

By Ella Rempel

Can a mother forget the baby at her breast and have no compassion on the child she has borne? Though she may forget, I will not forget you!

Isaiah 49:15 (NIV)

One reason I'm convinced of the testimonies of little children is that they eventually grow up to share them as adults. My wife's grandmother, Ella Rempel, was one such child. She carried her Jesus-story in her heart for many decades and finally shared it with me on her ninety-second birthday. She gave me permission to share it here.

A S A LITTLE GIRL of just six-years-old, I lived in Russia. For whatever reason, my natural parents gave me away to another family who took me reluctantly. No sooner had I moved in with my step-parents than the beatings began. For that first week, I was beaten every day with a stick, because, I was told, they were obeying the Bible's command to raise children very strictly. "Spare the rod and spoil the child," it says!

I learned quickly that the safest place to be was in my bedroom, which was really just a shed where the family kept their horse implements. Hanging above my little bed on the wall were reigns and straps used for the teams. I became so depressed that I wouldn't eat but my step-dad called me to the table and told me to sit. After we said grace, because of the beatings I had to ask, "Can I stand to eat? I can't sit." He replied, "You'll sit or I'll take you to the barn and give you such a beating that you'll have to sit." I took a spoonful of fried potatoes, said thank you for supper, and excused myself. I began to cry and cry until my step-mother said, "Your tears are falling all over the floor. If you don't stop, you'll be washing the floor with them." She had no sympathy at all. Then Step-dad said, "Pack Ella's things. I'm taking her back to her parents tomorrow." The next morning, I came to breakfast and had a little coffee made with wheat. Step-dad asked, "Is Ella packed?" His wife said, "There's nothing to pack. We're keeping her. I'll knock her parents right out of her so that she'll never even think of them."

The message that I heard from both families was, "We don't want you." In fact, my step-mother told me that I was so ugly, she didn't think that I'd even go to heaven. I was so upset that I thought my head was going to split. That night as I lay in bed, sinking into despair and wondering if God had abandoned me as well, something strange happened: The top seam of the peaked ceiling began to separate. The roof opened up above my head just like a zipper. Then the Lord came down through the roof and stood at the end of my bed. He was wearing a heavy kimono robe with a hood, which covered half his face. The light from the rest of his face was so brilliant that I couldn't see through it. But I could just see the glow of an eye. And he said, "You saw me!" He was so magnificent that I was filled with belief and a feeling of safety.

He looked all around the shed and then stretched his hand over the bed and said, "I will look after you." Then he touched my little foot. A white cloud of mist came over my bed, and all the strain went out of me. I felt a beautiful, warm sensation move up the whole length of my body, filling me with a wonderful peace.

Then he spoke to me very gently. The words have remained in my heart for my whole life. He said, "Ella, you will go to a different country and many very difficult things will happen to you. But I will be with you."

Then the Lord lifted himself slowly up through the roof and it came together perfectly. With that peace in my heart, I was able to fall asleep. The next morning when I went into the kitchen to wash, Step-mom looked at me, quite cross, and said, "Now where did you get that shine all over yourself?" I didn't tell her, but I never forgot. I knew then, "Even if I'm ugly, he came down to me." After that I always felt like he was nigh. Whenever I would ask for help, I knew he would take care of me.

• • • • • •

As Grandma Ella finished the story, she came back from that far away place and said to me with a smile, "And you know, he always did." As predicted, her step-family moved across the ocean, and Ella went through some unrepeatably hellish experiences. Having heard some of them, I am convinced that no explanation exists for her emotional health and utter lack of bitterness other than the reality of such a visitation. She suffered through it, survived, and overcame because Jesus came and suffered it with her.

17

Lilut

By Brad Jersak

A S THE SOLDIER PLAYED with the safety of his M-16 assault rifle, I thought I was going to be sick. It seemed like an awful nightmare, but I was awake—more fully awake than at any previous moment of my life.

It was November 1992. Desarmes, Haiti. After a *coup d'etat,* the paramilitary Macoutes no longer merely terrorized the countryside; they were actually running it. And they wielded an iron fist in this village in the Haitian outback. Groups larger than three could not meet without a permit. Youth groups and farmers' co-ops were forbidden. Checkpoints monitored traffic on the dirt roads.

Lares, a Haitian national serving the Mennonite Central Committee (MCC) as an agricultural trainer, had been arrested for allegedly distributing a disparaging letter against the local military chief. The soldiers had hog-tied him and beaten him with clubs about the head, ears, back, and thighs. Now they also declared their true intentions: "Tonight, we will get drunk and beat him to death. By morning, he will be dead. No bribe will change our minds."

Now Ron Bluntchly, our MCC host and guide, was standing face-to-face with an armed guard and speaking boldly in Creole: "God is your judge, and he is watching you! You must stand before him some day. He sees you now, and you will have to answer to him. He will hold you to account for this! He will not tolerate this injustice. Set this man free now!"

Questions began to race through my mind: Would they really kill Lares? Would they kill Ron? Would they dare? What about me? Could I escape with my wife, now six months pregnant? God? Where are you? What are you doing? What should we do?

As I listened, the Lord spoke:

"Is not this the kind of fasting I have chosen: *to loose the chains of injustice and untie the cords of the yoke, to set the oppressed free and break every yoke?* Is it not to share your food with the hungry and to provide the poor wanderer with shelter—when you see the naked, to clothe him, and *not to turn away* from your own flesh and blood?" (Isaiah 58:6–7)

God continued: "You can no longer spiritualize those verses away. This is very real, and it is *exactly* what Isaiah was talking about."

But how?

How could we liberate this literal prisoner, tied as he was in actual nylon cords, from an armed, flesh-and-blood oppressor? To break this stalemate would only serve to escalate the crisis, would it not?

Silence. I watched and waited, focusing on keeping my head and my bowels together. Ron would not back down. He believed that without witnesses like us around, the Macoutes would work up the courage to kill Lares. A crowd began to gather. Mugginess and tension weighed down on us. We cried out to the Lord in prayer, but despair threatened to win the day.

I was beginning to see through the blindness of those who accuse Christian organizations like MCC and Christian PeaceMaker Teams of being "too political." I had heard it before and even asked it myself: "Shouldn't they be restricting themselves to relief work or channeling their energies into 'soul-winning'? Why do they have to get so political?" In the Haitian context, where life and death stand out in stark contrast every day, *souls are people*. And the people are naked, starving, and oppressed. There is no fence of ambiguity to straddle. You can walk away in silent acquiescence to the misery and evil or you can speak out and act for justice and mercy, hoping to overcome evil with good. Sometimes being a follower of Christ leaves you no choice, regardless of what the critics believe.

In North America, we still don't understand this. Dom Helder Camara, the former Archbishop of Recife, Brazil once lamented, "When I gave food to the poor, they called me a saint. When I ask why the poor have no food, they call me a communist."

Now I was getting a crash-course on kingdom justice and mercy. I was coming to realize these are not merely temporal matters of politics or philanthropy that can be isolated from one's spiritual life. They are of eternal importance and will be addressed when Christ renders verdicts on Judgment Day. (cf. Matthew 25)

When the Day of Judgment comes, what we have done or neglected to do for the naked, the hungry, the prisoner, the sick, and the oppressed will be identified with what we did or did not do for the King. He will ask: "Did you feed me and clothe me or did you not? Did you welcome me, visit me, comfort me, free me, or not? You either came to me or abandoned me. If you helped them, you helped me. If not, I don't believe I know you."

On that day, whether we were "left" or "right" in our earthly politics will matter little when the divine judge beckons us to his left or his right. Whether we were conservative or liberal in our theology will flee from our minds. Even whether we said "the magic prayer" might seem shallow in that moment. But whether or not we did justice, loved mercy, and walked humbly with God will be of paramount concern (Micah 6:8). The New Testament teaches that we are saved by faith in the grace of God and not by good deeds (Ephesians 2:8–9). However, it also states that a truly living faith will not fail to reproduce the character of Christ in our lives, by which I mean our *actions* (James 2:26). It is not enough merely to listen to God. The ministries of Matthew 25 are not afterthoughts of Christian charity held in place with refrigerator magnets. They are the foundation of the very throne of God! "Righteousness and justice are the foundation of your throne; love and faithfulness go before you. Blessed are those who have learned to acclaim you, who walk in the light of your presence, O LORD" (Psalm 89:14). Once we have heard, we must follow through with action.

Lilut

Back to Haiti. As I stood there trembling, a little boy with a bright white, perfectly ironed shirt approached me. The boy, Lilut, was eleven-years-old, with dark black skin and bright white teeth. In the middle of this moment of hell, he smiled at me and began to rub my back. I saw Jesus looking at me through those big eyes. They said, *"It's going to be okay."*

Ron continued to lay his life on the line, demanding immediate release of the prisoner. The guard rebutted: "We cannot release him without a court order." What an odd "justice" system. You could arrest, sentence, and punish a man without so much as a warrant or any shred of evidence, but to free him required a trial.

"Then let's go to the judge," Ron countered.

"The judge is in the next town," the guard replied.

"Then we'll go to the next town."

"We have no truck."

Ron pulled out his keys. "We'll take my truck."

Under pressure from Ron, the foreign witnesses and the entire village, now the captors finally ran out of excuses. They loaded the prisoner and a handful of soldiers into the back of

Ron's pick-up and disappeared with Ron at the wheel. We waited and prayed that evening and throughout the night. What would happen? What if they didn't return? What would happen to Ron? What if the soldiers came for us next? What if…?

Eventually, the Lord broke through my troubled thoughts with his peace. In retrospect, was it God who suggested I have some dry bread with avocado to settle my stomach? I don't know, but it was a good idea, because after that I was finally able to get a little sleep.

The next morning, we heard the truck returning. Villagers poured out of their homes and lined the riverbed that doubled as their main road. The whole crew was returning, but now the ropes had been removed from Lares. He stood in the truck box smiling and waving at the crowds in this impromptu remake of Jesus' triumphal entry into Jerusalem. He was free! Men, women, and children began to chant in unison, "God is able! God is able!"

And there was Lilut, bright white eyes, teeth, and shirt, smiling at me through the dust. There was Jesus in our midst.

18

Allow the Poor Man to Save You

By Brita Miko

God sells righteousness very cheap to those who are eager
to buy: namely, for a little piece of bread, worthless clothes,
a cup of cold water and one coin.[1]

Abba Epiphanus

This began with a taste of heaven and hell. This began with a
taste of peace and torment. This began while giving birth to
my second child. The doctor broke my water just before 7 a.m.,
and my baby was born at 8:22 a.m. That final hour was contraction upon contraction. Labor is not the kind of pain that makes
you cry; it's the kind of pain that makes you gasp and writhe and
cry out "O God, help me!" It's also the kind of pain that makes

---

[1] Yushi Nomura (ed.), *Desert Wisdom: Sayings from the Desert Fathers.*
(Maryknoll, NY: Orbis Books, 2000) 101.

Kissing The Leper

you pass out—which I did, twice. Those unconscious moments of bliss during otherwise conscious pain were what started me thinking…

My assumption had always been that when you passed out, it was like falling asleep: Everything goes black, time continues without you noticing, and you are oblivious to everything outside of your dreams. This assumption turned out to be wrong. Everything did not go black when I passed out, but white. I was not oblivious, as I heard every word spoken by those around me. My husband, Pete, was calling gently to me, "Brita, Brita," and then he said, "I think she passed out." I was aware of my body— my head rolling slowly back and forth, my hand in his—but I could not feel any pain. Every nerve receptor seemed covered over, protected. I felt total peace. In a time of severe agony, I was experiencing a moment of grace. I knew Jesus was near. I knew he was right there. I could hear the doctor and nurse calling me out, saying I needed to wake up, but all I wanted was to stay. Forever. I had found rest, and I did not want to go back to the agony before me. And then, all at once, I was back. All the pain returned, and I was beyond the point where I could string a sentence together. My longing to return to that miraculous place of peace was so important I managed my one complete sentence, "I want to pass out again."

Later that day, after our little beauty had entered this world as the real miracle, it got me thinking about heaven and hell— one a place a rest, the other a place of pain—and how I had tasted both earlier that day. Two worlds came to mind as I lay in my hospital bed; two places where I remembered horror and bliss together.

The first world was a parable. In it are Lazarus and the rich man (Luke 16:19-31) and their revealed future destinies of peace and pain. It speaks of these places I have just tasted. Childbirth is an experience that underscores the fact that I do not want to be the rich man when the end comes. I do not want an eternity of contraction upon contraction. I want to understand this story and why Jesus created it and spoke it. The rich man is given good things, dies, and enters eternal torment. The poor man is given bad things, dies, and enters eternal rest. That's the simplest version. It has a hole. Rest, in this story, does not seem to be entered through Christ or forgiveness or grace. This troubles me, especially as I look at both of my beautiful girls and know that I have been given good things. I am not Lazarus. I am fearful and wanting to see Jesus in this story somewhere.

The second world that came to mind was the poorest community in Canada, Vancouver's Downtown Eastside. I remembered their stories and faces. There was my friend, Steve, who suffers from chronic back pain. He told me that when he was on heroin, all of his pain (physical and emotional) disappeared. He told me he would go from agony to peace. Heroin offered him a moment of rest. At the time his description of a heroin fix brought verses describing heaven into my mind.

I also remembered a young woman whose mind was often unaware of what she was doing. We were standing together on the street, and she was wearing socks with a pair of flip-flops jammed between her toes. She kept smiling and asking me if they looked pretty. I told her, "They look pretty." Later, she went missing. Later still, her DNA was found on accused serial killer Robert Pickton's farm (along with the DNA of at least 21 other women).

Lying in the hospital, I remembered a man who fought in Vietnam and returned with a gunshot wound and all the memories of the things he had done—and all the things that had been done to him—during the war. He came back and escaped his memories, for awhile. When I knew him, when my door was next to his, he was making it sober one day at a time. Carefully. Graciously. Mightily.

I also remembered this little man who tried to walk across the narrow brick pattern on the floor every day without stepping on any of the lines between the bricks. It was impossible, but his body would contort to perform it. During the soup kitchen meal he would only put one little pea in his mouth at a time. Each pea had to be eaten individually. He kept his face covered summer and winter. People whispered rumors he had been tortured, in another land, an earlier time.

Living and dead, they were among the poor of the earth.

There are all kinds of deep wounds and torment. There is pain that seems unending and perhaps unendurable. For spaces of time, the addicted escape through their use of heroin and cocaine. Moments of grace. Reprieve. Rest. I wondered if they (like me for that hour) have had glimpses into heaven and hell, peace and torment, with the distances between those extreme worlds separated by mere moments, seconds, breaths. I wondered at how desperately I wanted to return to unconsciousness during my very brief encounter with real pain.

In the story of Lazarus, the ones I met are the poor who receive bad things and die. I, with my new baby, look to Christ the Savior. I listen to his story. And I look for him in his story, for he is present in every moment. Where are you in this story of the rich man and Lazarus, where the outcome seems to depend, not on grace, but on circumstances or works or good and bad things?

And there he is. He's Lazarus. He's not just the one who received bad things; he received *every* bad thing. He's the one slapped, beaten down, busted up, and not just at Gethsemane or in some metaphorical way. If I grab your head and squeeze it and speak violently in your face, it is your face I am holding. But if I ask Jesus where he is, it's his face I hold, too. Every cruel act we do to each other, we are doing to him as well. He says, "Whatever you did to the least of these, you did unto me" (Matthew 25:40), because he inhabits them all. *Christ inhabits them all.* When Christ says, "When you visited the prisoner, you visited me," he isn't referring to some wrongly imprisoned innocent. He's referring to every menace to society; every one locked up or held for execution. Every one who is tortured. Every naked kid. Every one in socks and flip-flops waiting on the curb for her last ride.

For it isn't about a tally sheet at all. Did I feed enough orphans? Did I do enough hospital visitations? Rather, it is this:

Christ saves us. Christ in the poor man saves us. Christ in the
naked kid saves us. Christ in socks and flip-flops saves us. Our
encounters with such people change our hearts and lives. His
word to me is, "*Allow the poor man to save you.*" It feels like a
hard word, but he assures me it is easy if I will step out and try it.

In *Bono: In Conversation with Michka Assayas,* the lead
singer of U2 speaks about how he is holding out for grace, how
he needs grace, how he imagines God saying, "Let's face it,
you're not living a very good life, are you?" These words are for
me. These words are true. I like to think I do what I can for the
most part, but often I don't even do that. My life has not been
great. I have not been Mother Teresa. I have not been the hero
or the giant. I want to be saved through Christ, and I believe he
will save me. But sometimes he comes to me looking like the
one I most judge and most avoid. It is Jesus who saves and trans-
forms our hearts, and sometimes he does so in painful disguise.
Sometimes he looks disgusting or pitiful or worthy of contempt
or simply sick and tired and poor. But in receiving him, even in
these states, I find I am saved. In receiving him, I am changed.
Something happens to my heart, something good and *liberating*
and widening and beautiful. I don't need to feed the poor to be
good enough to get into heaven. But what am I to do? Believe
him. Follow him. Feed him. Eat him. Love him. Tend to his
sores. In doing so, I am always the one who has received, is receiving, will receive.

So, I asked Jesus the question, "When have I encountered
you?" and he started bringing people to mind, strangers I had

met. None of them were from the Downtown Eastside, however. This troubled me. So, I asked, "What about in the Downtown Eastside?" And he said, "*All of them.* Do you get it now? Whatever you did for the least of these, you did for me. It was me every time. I was every one of them. It was always me."

Abba Agathon

Going to town one day to sell some small articles, Abba Agathon met a cripple on the roadside, paralyzed in his legs, who asked him where he was going. Abba Agathon replied, "To town, to sell some things." The other said, "Do me the favor of carrying me there." So he carried him to the town. The cripple said to him, "Put me down where you sell your wares." He did so. When he had sold an article, the cripple asked, " What did you sell it for?" and he told him the price. The other said, "Buy me a cake," and he bought it. When Abba Agathon had sold a second article, the sick man asked, "How much did you sell it for?" And he told him the price of it. Then the other said, "Buy me this," and he bought it. When Agathon, having sold all his wares, wanted to go, he said to him, "Are you going back?" and he replied, "Yes." Then said he, "Do me the favour of carrying me back to the place where you found me." Once more picking him up, he carried him back to that place. Then the cripple said, "Agathon, you are filled with divine blessings in heaven and on earth." Raising his eyes, Agathon saw no man; it was an angel of the Lord come to try him.[2]

---

[2] Benedicta Ward (trans.), *The Sayings of the Desert Fathers* (Collegeville, MN Cistercian Publications, 1987), 21-22.

• • • • • •

see my face

I walk to a 24-hour corner store
east hastings and gore
12:30 in the morning
the air is raw
a hooker inside the place says
"can you buy me a cigarette?"

I do
and she tries to give me some change
I say "you asked me to buy it for you
        it's yours"

"thanks" she says and adds
"I got attacked tonight
 see my face"

she pushes back long brown strands of hair
 "two women jumped me"

I look at
the wounds
and blood
across her cheek and nose and ear and neck

"my old man was there" she says
"and he ran off and left me

he ran off with all my rent money
now I'm homeless
thanks for the cigarette"

and she walks away

the hebrews said you could not look
on the face of god
and live

but if you could
I think god's face
would look a lot
like hers

Bud Osborn
Used by permission.

Part 4

Joining Jesus
at the Open Table

Jesus was killed because of the way he ate.

R.J. Karris

The Father's House will open soon. My Table is going to be a very important place in the days to come. My people will have to understand the truths of Covenant and taste the fruits of genuine and intimate fellowship. I am going to send out a new revelation about My Table to my Bride, and she will sit with me at my Table and be healed. My House has room for all who come, and there will be a spread on My Table that has the capacity to feed the hungry.

Willy Soans
Prophetic Message
Nov. 9, 2000

19

Open Temple, Open Table

By Brad Jersak

And Jesus went into the temple of God, and cast out all them that sold and bought in the temple, and overthrew the tables of the moneychangers, and the seats of them that sold doves, And said unto them, It is written, My house shall be called the house of prayer; but ye have made it a den of thieves. And the blind and the lame came to him in the temple; and he healed them. And when the chief priests and scribes saw the wonderful things that he did, and the children crying in the temple, and saying, Hosanna to the Son of David; they were sore displeased, And said unto him, Hearest thou what these say? And Jesus saith unto them, Yea; have ye never read, Out of the mouth of babes and sucklings thou hast perfected praise?

Matthew 21:12–16 KJV

An Open Temple

O N THE DAY JESUS entered the outer courts of the temple and drove out the money-changers, he was not merely emptying the place. He was preparing to fill it. His assault was directed at the injustices of exclusion and spiritual abuse (cf. Matthew 21:13, Jeremiah 7:5–11). As author Steve Chalke says,

> The temple had become a huge filtration system for the religious leaders and chief priests to bar and exclude any who were deemed undesirable from access to God... For Jesus, although the temple was supposed to be "a house of prayer for all nations" (Isaiah 56:7) and a place of inclusiveness and welcome for all, it had become the exact opposite. It had become a symbol of Jewish exclusiveness and discrimination—and as such, it had to go![1]

What did Jesus see that day? The One, who for the love of the whole world, would open wide his arms on a cross in an invitation to all: What did the temple look like through his eyes? *What was he thinking?*

He saw the Holy of Holies, where all but the High Priest were excluded by an enormous curtain. *I shall tear that wretched veil in two and open that door permanently.* He saw the Holy Place, where only the priesthood could minister to the Lord. *I shall establish a priesthood for all who believe, where anyone can draw near with boldness.* He saw a wall of partition that excluded women, children, and Gentiles from the elevated place

---

[1] Steve Chalke, *The Lost Message of Jesus* (Grand Rapids: Zondervan), 105, 107.

(literally, by at least five meters) that only the men enjoyed. *I shall break that wall and flatten that floor. No one shall be outside or inside. No one shall be above or below.* He saw a gate guarded by "bouncers" who would use the threat of death to keep out all the disabled and the "sinners"—a technical term for those who had violated the holiness code and were unable to jump through the purification hoops, often because they simply couldn't afford it. *I shall create such a ruckus that even the lame and the sinners can slip in. I shall heal them and forgive them, cleansing them without any sacrificial offering but myself. And I shall do it now! I shall fulfill the word of the Lord through Isaiah:*

> "Make sure no outsider who now follows GOD ever has occasion to say, 'GOD put me in second-class. I don't really belong.' And make sure no physically mutilated person is ever made to think, 'I'm damaged goods. I don't really belong.'"

> For GOD says: "To the mutilated who keep my Sabbaths and choose what delights me and keep a firm grip on my covenant, I'll provide them an honored place in my family and within my city, even more honored than that of sons and daughters. I'll confer permanent honors on them that will never be revoked.

> "And as for the outsiders who now follow me, working for me, loving my name, and wanting to be my servants—All who keep Sabbath and don't defile it, holding fast to my covenant—I'll bring them to my holy mountain and give them joy in my house of prayer. They'll be welcome to worship the same as the 'insiders,' to bring burnt offerings and sacrifices to my altar. Oh yes, my house of worship will be known as a house of prayer for all people." (Isaiah 56:3–7 MSG)

And so, in they came. Immediately after cleansing the temple, see who enters: The least of these! First the blind, deaf, lame, and maimed. And Jesus begins to heal them all. And second, the children... LOUD children, crying out praises, refusing to be shushed. What a glorious bedlam of raw joy! What an affront to religious propriety! Poor Pharisees and priests, rushing around trying to regain control! But the damage was done. The healing meetings would carry on, and the old system would stay "offline" for the rest of the week. Only an execution could bring this anarchy to an end. End it? NO! In fact the Cross would establish it, nailing the written code that stood against us to the Cross forever (Colossians 2), opening the Holy of Holies for all time to all who would come (Hebrews 10), permanently erasing the division between Jew/Greek, male/female, and free/slave (Galatians 3)!

An Open Table

Historically, the centerpiece of Christian worship is no longer the Holy of Holies; it is the communion altar. The great drama of historical Christian liturgy rightly climaxes in the Lord's Table. What I find deeply troubling is how church leadership has progressively resurrected the exclusion of the temple system at the communion table. Rather than opening the table to all, the Church tends to restrict access to those considered to be "pure."

What does Jesus see when he looks at this situation? What does he think? Often, he sees an elite group (priests, deacons, males) reserving for themselves the right to serve communion.

He sees the communion table closed to all but "baptized members." He hears ministers serving up dire warnings of damnation to "sinners" who eat unworthily, encouraging those who are "not right" with the Lord or too young or outsiders to refrain from eating the bread and drinking the cup.

What we fail to notice is that the commonly used proof-text for this exclusion (1 Corinthians 11:20–34) specifies the "unworthy" as those who neglect others at the "Love Feast." Ironically, the Corinthians were celebrating the Body of Christ in the bread and wine while simultaneously abusing the Body of Christ in the people they treated as "less than." In a second, equally serious irony, we now use Paul's own words condemning exclusion from the table to reinforce our practices of exclusion from the table. Worse than merely guarding the temple doors, in closing the table, we are setting up religious hoops that keep "sinners" from free access to the broken body and shed blood of Christ. In such a scenario, who is eating and drinking unworthily?

I did not arrive at these conclusions theologically but by observing the work of Christ in, to, and through the least among us when we opened the table in our church. We did this because we sensed the Lord saying, "My house shall be a house of prayer for all" quite literally, and so we began opening our communion tables every week. At any point during the service, families, friends, and singles can make their way to the open table where they can receive prayer, anointing with oil, the laying on of hands, prophetic words, and the Lord's Supper. All who come are welcome to taste and see that the Lord is good. Those who serve at the tables can range from retired priests to youthful prophets to intercessors to people with disabilities to little children.

"Bobby"

What finally clinched my thoughts on the open table was an incident with Bobby, a fellow who loves to oversee the service from his wheelchair, which his careworkers park in the main entry (as gatekeeper) or on the stage (as bodyguard). Bobby usually communicates in whistles, laughs or shrieks. But he does know one word, and he can bellow it loudly. At any given moment, he shouts, *"HO!"* When he does, we delight to echo him.

One morning when Bobby said, "Ho!" I sensed the Lord saying, "He is announcing that the table is now open." Then Jesus brought to mind these words from Isaiah:

Ho! Everyone who thirsts,
Come to the waters
And you who have no money,

Come, buy and eat.
Yes, come, buy wine and milk
Without money and without price.
Why do you spend money for what is not bread,
And your wages for what does not satisfy?
Listen carefully to Me, and eat what is good,
And let your soul delight itself in abundance.
Incline your ear, and come to Me.
Hear, and your soul shall live;
And I will make an everlasting covenant with you—
The sure mercies of David. (Isaiah 55:1–3 NKJV)

In both Bobby and Isaiah (for they have the same Holy Spirit), God makes his invitation to the free and open meal of his eternal covenant with Jesus Christ, the Son of David. Now, whenever Bobby shouts, "Ho!" we remind everyone of that open invitation.

Inclusive Invitation/Exclusive Service

With all this talk of inclusion, am I saying that anything goes? That all parameters are stripped away? That *anyone* can eat? *Even the unbeliever?*

My belief is that ever since Jesus cleansed the temple, exclusion of anyone from his temple and his Table is completely out of bounds. The Lord's Table is for all whose souls are thirsty; for all whose sins and guilt need washing; for all whose bodies need healing—bar none (literally).

But not everything goes. Without standing as judge over other religions and their rituals, as a servant of Jesus Christ, I am only authorized to serve his menu. So all who come to the Table will know that we are serving forgiveness of sin and healing from brokenness that is available in the atoning work of Christ (Isaiah 53). This is what we offer... *Exclusively.* So it really is the Lord's Table: you won't find a deck of tarot cards, tea reading cups or statues of other gods. By being exclusive about *what* we serve, we can be inclusive to *whom* we serve. When I say, "This is the blood of Jesus for the forgiveness of sins," and then offer it freely, if the recipient partakes willingly in faith, is he or she not saying "yes" to the gospel itself? Or is this person not at least taking up the offer to taste and see that the Lord is good?

Love or Crack?

Christ's invitation to dine with him in table fellowship extended to society's most blatant pariahs. He had a reputation for being seen with tax collectors and prostitutes. He accepted their invitations and was frequently spotted on their turf. (The paparazzi would have loved it!)

My friend Nathan Regier pastors in Winnipeg at a church known for their unique motto: "Let worship and justice kiss." He loves to find the hidden value in those we think of as "at the bottom" and the hidden brokenness of those at the top, in places of power. Then they come together in community. They have made a ministry of partying with the "unpartyable"—those who are not allowed to be happy, experience pleasure or enjoy power.

Next door to their church is a hotel that functions largely as a crack house. Each resident has a bedroom, but generally it's treated like an open dorm of addicts, prostitutes and the very poor. In that place, Nathan and his interns encountered a woman in great distress. She was a prostitute with a crack habit and a bad debt to a local gang. She owed $20 plus interest, which happened to be $10 per day plus one beating per day. She was now up to $40 owing and had received two beatings.

The folks from Nathan's church bailed her out and began to treat her with love and dignity. They spoke to her about Jesus' love for her as an alternative to crack. She replied, "You talk to me about the 'love or crack' option, but crack is so easy to get and love is so hard to get." Seeing her dilemma they came up with a plan: Every day, some of the interns from the church would come and serve her the Lord's Supper and pray for the love of God to fill her and her little room. The goal was to accumulate such a sense of God's love and glory in the place that she could access it as quickly and easily as crack. Perhaps God's love plus the bread and wine would help her beat her habit.

As the group continued to minister communion daily in the prostitute's room, God's love began to make an impact. First, she became a Christian. Second, her crack use thinned from twice per day to twice per week. And third, other addicts and prostitutes began to gather about the door, asking for an invitation to the Table. Such an odd place for a communion altar—scandalous, even? But then again, remember the warning of Christ:

> I tell you the truth, the tax collectors and the prostitutes are entering the kingdom of God ahead of you. For John came to you to show you the way of righteousness, and you did not

believe him, but the tax collectors and the prostitutes did. And even after you saw this, you did not repent and believe him. (Matthew 21:32)

A Healing Table

The Lord's Supper is not just an open table. I believe it is also a healing table. In a mysterious but very real way, the presence of Christ is at the meal. (In the elements? In the act of partaking? In the person serving? All of the above?)

Of course, not everyone agrees with me. In a massive overreaction to the perceived "magic" of the Catholic doctrine of transubstantiation (belief in the literal transformation of the elements from bread and wine to flesh and blood), most Anabaptist streams asserted that the Lord's Table is "just a symbol."

I wonder how many times I heard that as a boy until I was finally convinced. *This is NOT his body. This is NOT his blood. This is just grape juice. (No wine allowed!) This is just bread. This is just a symbol. This is not a miracle. This is not a mystery. This is just a memorial. And now is the time where I beat myself up for my sins sufficiently until I'm worthy to eat these mere symbols. Luckily for me I'm not like those superstitious Catholics who actually believe they're drinking blood and chewing the literal flesh and bones of Christ.*

I continued to tell myself such things until one day, the mystery was gone and with it, the presence of Jesus. I would remember the history of Christ's sacrifice, but I didn't meet the living Jesus there anymore. Thankfully, the same churches gave me a love and trust for the Scriptures, where I read again, "This *is* my Body. This *is* my Blood." And "Unless you eat my flesh and drink my blood, you have no part of me." And "My flesh is real food and my blood is real drink!" (John 6) And so I began to believe again, not in something I could figure out, but in a mystery: that Christ is present at the table in a unique way. And I began to watch the table. Here is some of what I saw...

Quenton Wants a Cracker

The first time Quenton came to our church, we knew he might be a handful. He's a lovely man who suffers from autism and often seems tormented by memories of his time in an institution. He relives these experiences verbally, repeating disturbing phrases like, "Shut-up, Benson (his last name). The sticks are coming! The needles are coming!"

We also found out that he likes to interact with the preacher during the service. In a booming voice, he will say, "Shut up, preacher! Time to go home now!" (Usually, I think he's right.)

On his first visit to our church, Quenton was accompanied by his careworker, Priscilla. She had previous church experience, some of it quite bad. She was only along because her job required it, and I dare say she wasn't too happy about it.

Though he was fine during the worship time, Quenton became quite animated and noisy once Brian West, our speaker that morning, began to preach. But instead of treating this as a disruption, Brian began to interact with Quenton. At this point, Quenton became fixated on the communion table: "I want a cracker! I want a cracker!" Poor Priscilla was trying to restrain him, worrying about how we'd react. Instead, I snuck over to the communion table and took the plate to Quenton. He began to devour the whole thing in great handfuls, eventually settling down into a state of peace. I thought, "How nice. The crackers calmed him right down." But the Lord rebuked me, saying, "No. That was my *body* delivering him *peace*." His words jarred me. Perhaps some were offended by us opening the table to Quenton like this, but clearly Jesus was not.

A beautiful result of this first encounter was Priscilla's response. She said, "If this is how your church is going to treat

people like Quenton, I'm in." She started attending regularly, made her peace with God and the Church, and within about a year, became our youth leader and instigated a ministry to the poor called, "The Blessing Bag." Thanks Quenton!

A second incident involving Quenton and the table occurred a few years later. Some

"Quenton"

serious medical concerns had kept Quenton housebound and unable to attend church for about eight months. But during the Passion Week service, some careworkers chanced bringing him. At the outset, he was served communion and began to cry. This was notable, because someone who had worked with Quenton for ten years reported that not once had he ever expressed himself emotionally in this way. It was some sort of heart-level breakthrough (the violence also stopped as a result). The weeping continued for about twenty minutes, and then Quenton asked for me in specific to serve him communion a second time. After I served him, he settled down into his seat.

The service involved a mildly dramatic reading of the entire Passion narrative from Jesus' prayer in Gethsemene all the way to his resurrection. While I quoted the account of Jesus' arrest, Quenton became very upset and vocal. I read how Peter took out his sword and cut off Malchus' ear, and Quenton started shouting, "Leave the man alone! Leave the man alone!" Then Jesus replied, "Peter, put away your sword, for he who lives by the sword dies by the sword." Quenton sat back down and relaxed. The congregation was hushed, some of us weeping at this intimate interaction between Quenton and the Lord in Gethsemene.

I continued reading the crucifixion story. Between each of Jesus' sayings on the Cross, I paused for a moment of silence. During one of these silences, Quenton piped up clearly, "I want a drink of water. I want a drink of water." Then I read the next verse: "After this, Jesus knowing that all things were now accomplished, that the scripture might be fulfilled, saith, *I thirst.*" (John 19:28)

What was happening? I'm not certain, but I feel that Quenton received a healing at the table that allowed him to enter and experience the Passion narrative and to lead us into it with him. Just as marvelous was the aftermath in Quenton's health. The medical issues were sorted out and he was able to resume his outings.

Father Kornell

"Kornell"

As we kept watch for God's healing presence at the more-than-just-a-symbol communion table, the Lord sent us a retired Anglican priest. Kornell had become disillusioned with church and prayed, "Dad, I'm sick of church. I'm not going anymore." Yet just two years later, he found himself visiting us more and more frequently. Eventually, he committed to joining our prayer teams and serving at the Lord's Table.

The great thing about Kornell is that he already knows the truth of God's real presence when he offers the bread and the wine. As he serves the elements, he looks you in the eye and says, "This is the body and blood of Christ, broken and shed for you on the Cross. Now take it and rejoice, for you have died with Christ and have now risen with him." Then Kornell prays for the shalom wholeness of God to minister to the body, soul, and spirit of each person.

The result? On one occasion a little boy with a mysterious hip problem came to the table. The boy was limping with pain and unable to play soccer or hockey anymore. His parents couldn't trace the problem but came to the table where Kornell prayed for healing. The next morning, the boy woke up completely healed.

Shortly after that, a woman named Ruth came to the table. She is an amazing worship leader and pianist. But she was in tremendous pain with a "trigger thumb"—the ligaments were torn, some bones were fractured, and the joints were immobilized with bone chips. She couldn't bend it at all. The doctors couldn't cast it and estimated a minimum of eight weeks for it to heal, if at all. But she came to the table for prayer. She asked Kornell to pray, and he cupped her thumb in his own broken hands (crippled badly with arthritis). She wasn't able to hear anything he prayed, because the worship music was so loud. But within two hours, her thumb was completely healed.

The pain was gone, the mobility was back, and Ruth even had enough strength to give my wife a thirty-minute shoulder rub the following morning!

Allison

As much as I enjoy receiving communion from Kornell, my favorite meetings at the Lord's Table are with little Allison, a precious girl whose parents adopted her into their wonderful family. When she was only two, she was already serving communion with her mom. She would come to me and say, "You need prayer. I want to pray for you. I want to put oil on you." I would kneel in front of her at the table (or wherever she tracked me

"Ally"

down) and she would smear anointing oil on my forehead then lay her little fingers there and pray, sometimes in English, sometimes in another more angelic language. I would get blessed 100 percent of the time. The last time she prayed for me, a migraine I was suffering for several days disappeared in the space of about one minute. Alas, Allison and her parents have moved to another city where they will bless all those they touch. I might be a little bitter about the move. But I know we'll be sharing at the Lord's Table again some day.

As he did with his Father's temple, we believe that Christ has come to open his Table to all. The Lord's Table is more than just a symbol. It is a place where all who are thirsty and weak can come for a real encounter with the Living Christ and receive a gift of grace. The children and the childlike have taught us that such inclusion opens a path to healed hearts and healed bodies.

A Banqueting Table

So far, we've moved from the temple to the Lord's Table, but we must not stop there. The Eucharist is a spiritual portal into a much broader reality: the Kingdom of God as an open banquet, to which Christ has invited us all—especially the least among us.

All this talk of the open table ought to remind us of the many table meals that Jesus took during his ministry. The gospels record so many suppers that if Jesus' earthly ministry had come to my town, I'm quite sure his first order of business would have been choosing a restaurant, not a church! But it's not just where Jesus ate so much as who he ate with that created the great stir. Steve Chalke says it better than I:

> Mealtimes in first-century Palestine were microcosms of society as a whole. They had become social statements—and with whom you chose to share them was of great importance... The Pharisees thought of their dining tables as "little temples." They insisted on only eating with companions who had made themselves clean (i.e. persons in a state of ritual

purity; see Mark 7:2–4). It wasn't what you ate at these meals that was important; what mattered was with whom you ate.[2]

The Jewish table was as aggressive a caste system as any in the Middle Eastern world. Cross it, and you would be considered unclean, a sinner, merely by association.

Jesus' response is so contrary to such decorum that we must consider his actions and teachings around the table intentionally inflammatory—as "in your face" as the overturning of the temple tables. Socially, in fact, Christ was overturning the tables of religious and cultural exclusion on a continual basis. Meal after meal featured him with tax-collectors, prostitutes, and other sinners who quite enjoyed his company. The parties he attended opened him up to accusations of being a glutton and drunkard and (for shame) a friend of sinners (Matthew 11:19)!

> As he passed by, he saw Levi the son of Alphaeus sitting at the tax office. And he said to him, "Follow Me." So he arose and followed him.
>
> Now it happened, as he was dining in Levi's house, that many tax collectors and sinners also sat together with Jesus and his disciples; for there were many, and they followed him. And when the scribes and Pharisees saw him eating with the tax collectors and sinners, they said to his disciples, "How is it that he eats and drinks with tax collectors and sinners?"
>
> When Jesus heard it, he said to them, "Those who are well

---

[2] Steve Chalke, Ibid, 158.

have no need of a physician, but those who are sick. I did not come to call the righteous, but sinners, to repentance." (Mark 2:14–17 NKJV)

Far from fearful of somehow being infected by them, Jesus believed that his presence might even "spike" the food and wine with some healing love. The Pharisees thought repentance preceded relationship: You have to be clean, then you can join in and get touched by God's love (just as at the temple). Jesus saw it the other way around: You come and join in close enough to get cleansed by God's touch. In fact, by dining with sinners, Christ was declaring them clean. This is why Jesus not only pursued supper in the outcasts' homes (Remember Zacchaeus?), he also requires us to do the same.

> # By dining with sinners, Christ was declaring them clean.

Then Jesus said to his host, "When you give a luncheon or dinner, do not invite your friends, your brothers or relatives, or your rich neighbors; if you do, they may invite you back and so you will be repaid. But when you give a banquet, invite the poor, the crippled, the lame, the blind, and you will be blessed. Although they cannot repay you, you will be repaid at the resurrection of the righteous."

When one of those at the table with him heard this, he said to Jesus, "Blessed is the man who will eat at the feast in the kingdom of God." Jesus replied: "A certain man was preparing a great banquet and invited many guests. At the time of the banquet he sent his servant to tell those who had been invited, 'Come, for everything is now ready.'

"But they all alike began to make excuses. The first said, 'I have just bought a field, and I must go and see it. Please excuse me.' Another said, 'I have just bought five yoke of oxen, and I'm on my way to try them out. Please excuse me.' "Still another said, 'I just got married, so I can't come.'

"The servant came back and reported this to his master. Then the owner of the house became angry and ordered his servant, 'Go out quickly into the streets and alleys of the town and bring in the poor, the crippled, the blind and the lame.'

"'Sir,' the servant said, 'what you ordered has been done, but there is still room.'

"Then the master told his servant, 'Go out to the roads and country lanes and make them come in, so that my house will be full. I tell you, not one of those men who were invited will get a taste of my banquet.'" (Luke 14:12–24 NIV)

What if Jesus really meant this? What if he meant this at the social level, calling his disciples to actually obey his injunctions regarding social gatherings? What if, instead of having our private parties and then serving the leftovers to the food bank, we were to actually dine together with the least of these? In Jesus' mind, high-end accountants are found asking the homeless to pass the butter. The Ph.D. wipes the chin of the paralytic who can't keep it all in. The addict and the worship leader talk and laugh and share together. The only prerequisite to joining the family meal is saying "Yes!" to the invitation.

And what if Jesus sees this as indistinguishable from the gospel banquet? That is, as you join the earthly love feast with friends who welcome you to eat with them, you find yourself entering God's family and tasting the goodness of God at "the table prepared for you." What if that even led progressively to your salvation?

This I have against you

I am beginning to see this happen in our faith community. A few years ago, I asked the Lord for a letter to our church like those in the book of Revelation, each of which included an affirmation, a criticism, and a promise.

In our case, when it came time for the critique, I sensed God saying, "Your church has been meeting for over five years, but you still haven't become a family. And every time I tell you that, you have a barbecue, but it's not working."

His words stung with the prick of truth. Anyone who was wounded or prickly or even sleepy would slip into church late and make a quick exit at the end. They could come for years without plugging into a relationship. The barbecues were too small, too few, and too far between. When we tried an after-church lunch, numbers were small.

The leadership went to prayer, and God led us to start a monthly "Soup Sunday." After thirty minutes of worship and a very brief message or testimony, we launch into a potluck soup buffet, not *after* the service, but *as* the service. At first, people huddled with family and close friends. But over time, social barriers began to crumble like crusty rolls. Conversations led to relationships and behold, a family began to grow! As those who deemed themselves "sinners" realized they were loved and not condemned, they found it safe to invite others to the banquet. Relationships led to healings, which somehow led to baptisms. Don't ask me how. Somewhere between the Pho or Borscht and the baptismal waters, I lost track. It has something to do with God's love and the fact that *anyone* can come to our soup table, and therefore *anyone* can come to God's banqueting table.

> ## "He takes in sinners and eats meals with them, treating them like old friends."
> ### Luke 15:2 (MSG)

The Christian Satanist?

One day I noticed a fellow I'll call Clark at Soup Sunday. This surprised me for two reasons: First, because I was told he led the Satanist club at the local university. Second, because I had passed him on my way to church, which made me realize he had walked several miles across the city to join us. I know Clark from the coffee shop that we both call our second home, and we have some mutual friends. He's a good guy and a great rapper. It was great that someone invited him to our humble banquet and that he'd made such an effort to RSVP in person. And I was impressed that instead of responding to him with a wide berth and spiritual warfare incantations, our people filled his table and seemed sincerely glad to share a meal with him. In fact, before long Clark became one of "our people" as well.

In short, there was no dramatic conversion story with which to send him out on the conference circuit. Rather, Clark began to attend monthly, then when he could, weekly. He's on his own faith journey like the rest of us, but we get the benefit of his company. I don't know how you feel about breaking bread with a "Christian Satanist," but I can tell you this: One year after he started coming, Clark delivered a profoundly prophetic rap song to conclude the worship set at our Easter service, and he sounded a lot more like Jesus than Anton LaVey. He followed that up by giving me a gift: a classic, hardcover edition of Brother Lawrence's *Practice of the Presence of God.* He didn't realize that when we have a coffee together, I am doing that already.

Yes, and the Bisexual, Too

Jill (not her real name) had been coming to Fresh Wind for about a month when she finally approached me for a coffee meeting. She wanted to know how I felt about gays, lesbians, and bisexuals. Specifically, if I knew that someone was gay, would he or she still be welcome in our church? After a series of very hurtful experiences, she needed to know how I would "deal with her."

The first thing that came to mind was that in the gospels, Jesus never addressed homosexuality directly. But we do know from Mark 2 that many "sinners" were among his disciples.

You'll remember that the title "sinner" encompassed all those who fell short of the Levitical holiness code, which happens to condemn homosexuality. Based on that, of course she's welcome at our table. For it is only at the Table that anyone is made whole. So I took this approach:

"Jill, I'm not going to quote Bible references at you. No doubt, you've heard them already. I'm going to use you as my reference point. If you feel that your bisexuality is sin and bondage and if you think you need to walk through repentance and deliverance, I'm willing to walk with you. If you feel that it's a type of brokenness, a symptom of past abuse that needs inner healing, I'm willing to walk with you. And if you feel that God made you this way and you just need to know he loves you and that we won't reject you, I'm happy to walk with you. All I ask is that we could talk to Jesus together about it. My job is not to be your judge. My job is to help you hear God's voice and to feel his love."

Jill replied, "Well that's the thing. I *do* have hurts from the past, but every time I bring that up, the pastor says, 'Aha! See! That's the problem!' But I don't believe that's the problem. I don't believe there *is* a problem."

"Well, I'm not going to do that to you," I assured her, "If you want to look at your healing issues on their own without me pushing you about your sexuality, that's totally okay. But can we talk to Jesus about it together?" She was agreeable to this, so we bowed right there, and I asked God to show her that perfectly safe place in her heart that God had preserved from darkness, abuse, or defilement—the place in her heart where he would want to meet and tell her about his love for her. Immediately, she saw herself with her dad (a safe person to her) in a fishing boat on a lake surrounded by forest on top of a mountain. It was completely peaceful.

I asked Jill where Jesus was in that picture. She said that he filled the entire scene with his presence. He was everywhere. I asked Jesus to tell her about his love for Jill. She told me, "I can't hear any words, but every sound in the whole forest is telling me how much he loves me." At this, she began to weep. She could actually feel God's love filling her, and it was overwhelming. I suggested that she just bask in his love for a while. Finally, I asked Jesus if there was some healing work that he wanted to do. He told her, "No. I just want to love you for a while," to which she responded by weeping some more.

That was a Thursday. On the following Sunday, Jill came to church and returned to that picture as an aid to worship. She closed her eyes, stood up with hands raised, and felt the love of God flooding into her again as she entered the vision. Her praise was free and genuine. When she opened her eyes, she was surprised to see a little girl (who looked suspiciously like her as a child) staring up at her with a big smile. Just then, the Lord whispered to Jill, "I'd like you to be a mom someday." That caused a serious double-take, because, as she said, "It was so random!" But this wasn't a demand. It was God's heart, and it touched her heart. This set her to pondering.

I didn't really follow up with Jill for a while, because God's instructions were clear. Until further notice, his plan was merely to love her. When Jill asked for another appointment, she opened by saying, "I've met the man who will be my husband. I'm in love, and he's in love, and we both love God. We plan to get married this spring."

I can hear the chorus of "What about's...?" and unresolved issues and "Yes, but where do you stand when...?" In other words, "Why does your teacher eat with tax collectors and 'sinners'?" (Matt. 9:11)

Jesus has already addressed all of these questions:

"It is not the healthy who need a doctor, but the sick. But go and learn what this means: 'I desire mercy, not sacrifice.' For I have not come to call the righteous, but sinners." (Matt. 9: 12-13)

I figure I'll just let Jesus guide Jill's journey while I encourage her to keep coming to the table to listen to him. His wisdom has taken her further along than any of my arguments and phobias could ever do. For now, my point is this: God's banqueting table is open and he's commanded us to invite everyone: the poor, the sick, the sinner, and the ones that the Church labels as the least or the lost. We aren't called to make them do anything before they get to Jesus or his open table. We just need to bring them to the One who offers an overflowing cup of goodness and mercy (Psalm 23). Once they taste it, you never know what miracles will result.

20

A Yummy Password

By Eric Kuelker

IN MAY OF 2004, I was sitting on the kitchen floor when my two-year-old daughter Lauren started walking through the kitchen. I reached my hands out to her and started calling to her, "Lauren, Lauren, come to Daddy, Lauren." Nothing. She kept on walking without even so much as a glance in my direction. She passed within six inches of my toes and continued on to the dining room. In that moment I realized there was something very, very different about my daughter. Four months later, after tests and delays, Lauren was diagnosed with infantile autism.

In the ensuing months, we were filled with the deep pain of acknowledging Lauren's condition, and much anxiety. During this time, the BC government won a decision in the Supreme Court that meant they would not have to pay the full cost for treating autism. Thus, we had to face the fact that Lauren's

$25,000 annual treatment would have to come out of our pockets. In addition to this stressor, I also had considerable conflict with my work over a contract dispute.

The night of December 12, 2004 was an awful night. I awoke at 4:00 a.m. filled with anxiety about this and other con-

"Lauren"

flicts at my workplace as well as how I was going to provide for my family. I could not fall back asleep no matter how much I prayed, read my Bible, did relaxation exercises, etc. As the minutes of the night ticked away, I cried out to God for him to speak to me.

We stumbled into church later that morning. Soon after the service started, Lauren grabbed my finger and towed me right to the communion table. The plates were covered with a cloth, and she fussed at one that was covering the bread. I uncovered the plate, and she immediately took a piece of bread, dipped it in the juice, looked me in the eyes, and put it in my mouth. I was amazed. One of the core symptoms of autism is lack of social interaction. Not only was she feeding me, she was looking into my eyes, far more than she ever did at home. She did this four times. The symbolism of the number four was not lost on me as I felt it referenced my 4:00 a.m. worries. When Lauren was finished, she grabbed my finger, towed me away from the communion table, and we sang. Each time we sang the word "light," she stepped forward to peer closely at the nearby candles. While looking at the candle, she said "I know is hot." This was the longest and most sophisticated sentence she had ever spoken.

Half an hour later, she grabbed me by the finger and towed me over to the second communion table. She picked up a piece of bread, dipped it in the wine, and fed me. Again. And again. And again. She fed me the entire plate of bread. A piece fell on the floor. I discreetly set it on a basket, and she bent down, picked it up, and fed it to me, too. Then she grabbed a cup of wine (shot glass size). She tasted it then held it up to my mouth and poured it in. She picked up the next glass, and poured it in my mouth. She kept on pouring wine in until I had to stop her because I was getting light-headed! My throat was tight with emotion from having my autistic daughter interact so much with me and by the unique way she had found to bless me.

But God had just gotten started.

At the end of the service, I asked the pastor to pray for me. As he was praying, my four-year-old son Matthew was hanging around. Afterwards, Matthew and I walked past the communion table to our seats. He asked if he could have some. I said sure. I told him that this was the body and blood of Jesus that he gave us

on the Cross. He said "I know, Dad." Then he reached for the
bread, caught himself, stopped, bowed his head, and said, "Dear
Jesus, we thank you for the Cross and we ask to walk on your
path, amen." That was the first time he had ever spontaneously
initiated prayer. Then he proceeded to eat all the bread on the

"Jillaine"

plate. He turned to me and said "The more we eat, the more we
are blessed." I stared at him and asked, "Who told you that?" He
said "God did. It's a yummy password!"

Then he reached for a cup of juice and drank it down. He
looked at me and said "The more we drink, the more we are
blessed." I asked, "Who told you that?"

"God did," he said. "He gave me two yummy passwords today!" Then Matthew bounced his way up the aisle, turned and shouted again, "Two yummy passwords!"

Tears filled my eyes.

It was not until an hour later that all the implications unfolded for us. My wife commented that Lauren's actions, of dipping bread into wine and feeding it to me, were just like the ceremony of the priest feeding his people communion in the Catholic Church. I recognized that my daughter had demonstrated the principle that the more we eat of Christ, the more we are blessed, by feeding me all the bread and wine available. My son not only repeated the principle in his actions but he articulated it so that even I could understand. Then he emphasized that it was a password by which we access the hidden treasures of God's Kingdom.

As I tucked Matthew and Lauren in that night, I was especially grateful that God had placed them in my life, for how they blessed me so richly. When I looked at Jillaine, Lauren's twin sister, my attitude was a little different. I saw her as… well, just a little different. As being slightly behind her siblings, a tiny bit second-rate. God had spoken so clearly through Matthew and Lauren but not through her.

God must have chuckled at this wisp of judgment. The next Sunday, the service was nearly over, and Jillaine saw me singing near the communion table. Suddenly, she was by my side holding two communion cups. "Here, Daddy," she said, and handed me a cup. We prayed, drank it together, and I kissed her, and returned to singing. She bounced up again with two more cups. We shared those. She did it again. Brad, our pastor, came up to me and started chatting about what happened the previous Sunday with Lauren and Matthew when Jillaine appeared again with two more cups, each dripping slightly. With a start, I realized it was happening all over again! Without any prompting, Jillaine brought me every single cup of juice on the communion table for the two of us to live out the principle that the more you eat and drink of Christ, the more you are blessed. It was an extra joy for me that God revealed to all three of my children that we are all equally his priests in God's kingdom.

21

Stray Dogs or Royal Children?

By Brad Jersak

The Story of Mephibosheth

One day David asked, "Is there anyone left of Saul's family? If so, I'd like to show him some kindness in honor of Jonathan." It happened that a servant from Saul's household named Ziba was there. They called him into David's presence. The king asked him, "Are you Ziba?" "Yes sir," he replied. The king asked, "Is there anyone left from the family of Saul to whom I can show some godly kindness?" Ziba told the king, "Yes, there is Jonathan's son, lame in both feet." "Where is he?" "He's living at the home of Makir son of Ammiel in Lo Debar." King David didn't lose a minute. He sent and got him from the home of Makir son of Ammiel in Lo Debar. When Mephibosheth son of Jonathan (who was the son of Saul), came before David, he bowed deeply, abasing himself, honoring David. David spoke his name: "Mephibosheth." "Yes sir?" "Don't be frightened," said David. "I'd like to do something special for you in memory of your father Jonathan. To begin with, I'm returning to you all the properties of your grandfather Saul. Furthermore, from now on you'll take all your meals at my table." Shuffling and stammering, not looking him in the eye, Mephibosheth said, "Who am I that you pay attention to a stray dog like me?" David then called in Ziba, Saul's right-hand man, and told him, "Everything that belonged to Saul and his family, I've handed over to your master's grandson. You and your sons and your servants will work his land and bring in the produce, provisions for your master's grandson. Mephibosheth himself, your master's grandson, from now on will take all his meals at my table." Ziba had fifteen sons and twenty servants. "All that my master the king has ordered his servant," answered Ziba, "your servant will surely do." And Mephibosheth ate at David's table, as one of the royal family. Mephibosheth also had a small son named Mica. All who were part of Ziba's household were now the servants of Mephibosheth. Mephibosheth lived in Jerusalem, taking all his meals at the king's table. He was lame in both feet.

2 Samuel 9:1–13 MSG

IS IT ALREADY TWO YEARS since I visited the Hand–Crafter? It's a facility in Boissevain, Manitoba, Canada, where people with various disabilities gather to create quite stunning crafts while encouraging one another in community. (Check out their catalogue at www.handcrafter.ca.) While there, at least twenty individuals passed around my laptop computer in order to see a colorful slideshow of my family and friends. They treated me to some snacks, and then we opened the Bible together for a little chat.

Reading 2 Samuel 9 with them was a powerful experience, because it begins with a real king—King David, no less—summoning an individual with a disability. (In the old days we'd say, "a cripple." The language keeps changing, so please pardon my lingo.) The group imagined together how exciting that would be. I must say, the childlike enthusiasm made it difficult for some to stay seated or refrain from shrieking. And why should they?

But then we came to this awful statement where Mephibosheth demeans himself, saying *"Who am I that you pay attention to a stray dog like me?"* Of course, it's a rhetorical question, and he probably expected the same answer he must have heard repeatedly throughout the years, "You're no one, a nobody. You're not worth slowing down to attend to, much less receive the attention of a king."

Where did Meph (for short) get the label, "stray dog?" Had he concluded that himself? Or were labels like that put on him by those who dehumanized him?

That's where I made my big mistake. I asked the Hand Crafters that question. They answered firmly, from experience, "NO! It was other people. The people on the street who *say things. Rude things!*

"Like what?" I asked.

"Like 'stupid,'" said one. "And 'dummy,'" cried another, jumping to his feet . "Slow. Idiot! Retard! *Retard!* RETARD!"

They said, voices breaking. Tears came. Anger arose. I figured it was very cathartic if it didn't trigger seizures or a full-scale riot.

By now all of us were crying. (And now I'm crying again as I write this. You may be crying as well, which is good.) Very upsetting. Time to rescue it. I showed them how David put a stop to such talk.

"NO! You are not a stray dog. You are not stupid, not a dummy, not a retard! I take those labels off you. You are NOT your disability, NOT your diagnosis, NOT your syndrome! Your identity must no longer revolve around your condition. From this day forward, you will dine at the king's table as one of his own sons. Do you hear me? You are NOT a dog. You are a SON!"

I looked at each of the sons and daughters in the shop. They were holding their breath. And I asked, "Does anyone know what you call the son of a king?" A young man replied, "A prince?"

"That's right. And who can tell me what the king's daughter is called?" A young lady responded, "A princess!"

"Yes. And did you know that Jesus is a King? And that he has a banqueting table? And that he has invited all of you to join him? That today he says, 'YOU are my son. YOU are my daughter. YOU are my princes and princesses! All are welcome!'"

To say that the room went ballistic right then would not do it justice. Joy burst out as the revelation hit home. They began to describe with gusto what royal children wear: crowns, tiaras, jewels, robes, and staffs. I dare say I saw the swagger of kings in many that day. I saw the royal blood of Christ setting some things straight.

• • • • • •

Who am I in all of this? Lord, can I be like Ziba in this story? Grant that I and my children and their children should serve royalty such as Mephibosheth and the Hand–Crafters all the days of our life. Let us ride their coat tails into the banqueting hall of your Kingdom.

Final note: Ponder the last phrase of the final verse. Having reported this transformation from dog to prince, the narrator reminds us, "By the way, did I mention that he was crippled in both feet?" Did he miss God's whole point? Couldn't he resist leaving the label in the dust bin? Why is that the final word?

How often do we make this same mistake? I am reminded of the great care we take to use politically correct language: *"Please don't call them 'disabled'... Now we simply call them 'individuals.'"* But then when it comes to sharing their testimonies, using their names, and showing their pictures, we walk a fine line because these "individuals" are *"legally incompetent."* So, to avoid trouble and red tape, we're tempted to simply change their names and delete their photos, thus making them nameless and faceless once again.

We replicate this error in the broader church as well. We welcome people to a new life covered by grace where the old is gone and everything is new... But then we can't resist recalling and reminding them of their past and their old labels. Far better to simply take up the mantle of Ziba and serve them as children of the king.

22

Open Arms, Open Heart

By Brad Jersak

Sometimes the body knows what the mind cannot believe.

John Van Vloten

ANNA WEIGHED LESS than seventy pounds when I first met her. She was fighting a losing battle with anorexia and bulimia. Body systems were shutting down. Her bio-thermostat and reproductive systems were already offline, her heart was racing, and her digestive system was messed up. She ate like a bird but felt that even adding cream to her coffee was disgusting. She would throw up anything she ate about five times daily. Now this precious nineteen-year-old was under a doctor's death sentence: "If something doesn't change, you will be dead in nine months."

Her pastor was pleading with me to see Anna (not her real name), even for an hour. Aware that I could do nothing in an hour and hesitant to open such a can of worms, I said a grumpy "No Way!" After further pleading, I answered, "Phone her and ask directly, *Do you want to be free?* If Anna gives you a direct 'Yes,' then I'll see her for an hour." I confess that my heart was cold enough and my eyes dry enough to hope she would refuse. But shortly afterwards, I received a phone call that led to my first face-to-face encounter with Anna.

A bit of back-story: Why my callous response? At the time, I was suffering the effects of some inner vows. In trying to help and pray with others through similar issues, I found myself to be a bit of a rescuer, and that led to some serious disappointments and issues of transference. From there, I hardened my heart with the assertion, "I'll never let that happen again." As they say, "Once bitten, twice shy."

So for several years, when I did pray with others, I would try to be kind, but I certainly wouldn't allow myself feelings of compassion or love for fear of becoming confused or causing confusion. Tears and empathy were certainly put away. I reasoned that this was supposed to be all about God and not about me. I'm not the Savior. I'm not the Healer. He is.

What I didn't realize was that shutting my heart to the love of God for others affected me across the board. It unplugged part of my heart from God, from my wife Eden, and from my children... and I didn't even notice. It also damaged my spiritual eyes. I didn't see others as God does, because I felt I mustn't. It might stir up emotion and even break my heart.

Meanwhile in the natural world, I had just received laser eye surgery, and it hadn't gone very well. My vision was regressing, and my eyes were extremely dry. I was complaining about this to God, and he responded, "That's right. Your eyes have regressed. And they *are* very dry. Did you notice that you're the only teacher in your church that never weeps when he preaches? Did you notice that the verse, 'Weep with those who weep' doesn't seem to apply to you?"

I got the point. I countered, "Well, I can't make myself cry, and I'm not going to fake it. If you want me to feel more, then you'll have to do something in my heart." That conversation took place the morning of the day I met Anna.

• • • • • •

The moment I saw Anna, my heart turned. I felt a sense of compassion in my gut that scared me. It felt like love—like being *in love*. Not sexual attraction; not the temptation of lust. I saw a little girl who looked like an Auschwitz survivor. (Sorry, Anna, but it *was* startlingly harsh then.) She stumbled in on spindly legs that buckled as she walked. The pastor, a caring lady who has carried Anna's burden for miles in prayer, sat next to Anna on the floor as I took a seat across from them. I asked her a few questions, trying to connect, and then the Lord spoke to my heart in loud, clear tones (no still small voice this time): "Hold her!" Shocked, I voiced my objections immediately, "NO WAY! This is a nineteen-year-old woman! I've already botched my way through transference at least once! Do you want me to get sued?"

It's the only time I remember God ever raising his voice at me. "GET OVER YOURSELF! People are dying!" Then more calmly, "You've done well in departing from those profession-

"*Anna*"

als who attempt to heal without the Cross. So why are you copying their attempt to heal without love? And besides, it's not THAT hard to make it safe."

Sheepishly, I asked Anna if her pastor and I could each sit on one side of her with arms around her. She consented and we spent the next few hours praying through some of the core hurts that drove her illness. Mainly, I would just lay hands on her bony shoulders or her protruding spinal column and quietly try to let the love I felt in my heart drain into her body. I had a clear sense that my prayers were shallow but that God's love could touch her at a level where nothing but love works. I prayed meat onto her bones and asked for healing for her heart. God spoke to her that evening and promised that she would not die, that she would live to sleep under the Christmas tree the following year.

That Sunday morning, when I preached in her church, I began to weep. Tears came, but I didn't care. My experience with Anna had opened up some sort of emotional spring. It opened even wider when, out of the corner of my bleary eye, I saw Anna *running* over with a tissue so I could wipe my tears. I realized then that she was Jesus, healing me of my dry eyes and hard heart. For that, I'll always be grateful.

Over the next week, without changing her behaviors, Anna gained ten pounds! By the end of the next month, her body systems were working again. Another couple of months in and she had gained thirty pounds. When her doctor asked about this remarkable progress, she testified that Jesus was healing her as she listened to him and let him love her.

Since then, there have been some ups and some steep downs, but I remain confident that Anna is going to make it. Others have come alongside her, and I trust that God will complete what he started in her AND in me. He is restoring her heart and making her beautiful. "The one who calls you is faithful and he will do it" (1 Thess. 5:22). I leave her story with a poetic prayer that she sent to me in the midst of her struggle—a prayer that I believe Jesus is still answering:

she sits in her chair
so scared and unaware
of what could happen any second now
take her hand here and now

Jesus can you hold me
can you take away my pain
i know you can and will
if only my pride i'd slain

a little girl's tears
from everything she fears
a nurse holds her hand and says "it's okay"
but she knows inside that it won't go away

Jesus, can you hold me
can you help me just let go
i know you can and will
if this burden on you i will bestow

this girl sits up in bed
scared to death of what they said
not much longer to wait
until she'll stand at the pearly gates

Jesus, can you hold me
i dont know how to give up
i know you won't let go
the love that only you show

she could have had life
but so much pain and strife

took over her body and she closed her eyes
to her mother and father's horrible surprise

Jesus, you are holding me
i see you so clearly now
how could i have been so blind
so much i left behind...

as many love and hugs that i can gather,
tears fall from my face,
but i'll still be here loving you,
thanks for being a best friend...
loving me, fairy dust, and angel wings, in dreams,

Anna

• • • • • •

This, however, is not where *my story* ends. That same weekend, I went to visit my parents and encountered a second cousin of mine for the first time. She was about eight-years-old and full of life: big brown eyes and mischievous freckles! On the other hand, she lives with a single mom, and her father only makes contact with her once a year, usually by phone. As she goaded me to play with her, I could feel her need for male physical touch. The voice came again, "Love her. Play with her. And be VERY physical. Tickle her, wrestle with her, cuddle her."

Again I balked. "But Lord, I'm scared. I'm NOT her dad and I won't be around for her after tomorrow. Don't you know how people see 'uncles' these days? Don't you know about the scandals with religious leaders and children? I'm not interested in any appearance or accusation of pedophilia!" Fear threatened to undo the recent softening of my heart.

God's correction came swiftly. "What are you saying? That she should never feel *clean* physical touch from males? What if experiencing clean touch from you is how she will learn to discern between love and abuse? Would you really protect her from abuse by withdrawing all healthy male affection?" Then came the same gentle follow-up, "Besides, her mother is right beside you; your brother and dad are right in front of you. There are ways to make this safe for her and for you."

I gave in... in fact, my newly softened heart was glad to surrender. As I took this little princess onto my lap, out of the blue she asked, "Could you teach me how to hear God?" I said, "No. You already know. I'll show you." I prayed aloud, asking God to tell her how he felt about her and how he saw her. Then I said to her, "Now listen with your heart. What's he saying?" She quickly tuned into that voice by which we learn of God's love. She was flabbergasted by God's delightful answers, and her eyes filled with tears to hear of his love directly. She moved quickly to listening for others. She heard beautiful words of encouragement for her mother. Then she interrupted herself and said to me, very seriously, "Jesus is telling me that a tornado is coming to your life. But he says, 'Don't worry. I will dig a hole for you and hide you in it. It won't hurt you.'" I was taken aback. I've already learned to listen carefully to what Jesus is saying through children, but this was more than that. Two mature intercessors had independently given me virtually the same message with the same imagery during the previous weeks! The same Spirit was speaking through this little girl just minutes into her first lesson in listening to God.

So, for the second time that weekend, by taking a little risk of love to be Jesus to someone, he had now reversed the flow and was ministering to me through them.

By the way, the impending "storm" came as foretold, but so did the promised shelter. As Jesus said,

> Howbeit when he, the Spirit of truth, is come, he will guide you into all truth: for he shall not speak of Himself; but whatsoever he shall hear, that shall he speak: *and he will shew you things to come.* (John 16:13 KJV)

Throughout the next month, I found out that God is very interested in *our* love for others, not just his own love. God the Father spoke to my heart saying, "When I love someone, I don't merely want you to be a passive witness of my love. I want a piece of your heart. I want you to love with my love, because some things can only be healed with love. And, more importantly, I want your heart to be like mine. Stop trying to avoid falling in love. Love everyone. Fall in love with everything. Evangelicals have so obsessed over the overuse of "love" language that they're becoming loveless. Go ahead, love your wife and children; fall in love with all the baristas at the coffee shop and with the vanilla lattes they serve; with all the customers that come in and with their haircuts, their tattoos, their unique fashions. Fall in love with the grass and the rain outside, with mountain flowers and glaciers! Your problem has NEVER been that you love too much. That is NEVER why you struggle or stumble. Go ahead and love... I want to give you a heart big enough to encompass the world. I want to give you MY heart."

Surprisingly, within days of hearing these words, I read the following passage from Fyodor Dostoyevsky cited in Richard Rohr's *Everything Belongs:*

> Love people even in their sin, for that is the semblance of Divine Love and is the highest love on earth. Love all of God's creation, the whole and every grain of sand of it. Love every leaf, every ray of God's light. Love the animals, love the plants, love everything. If you love everything, you will perceive the divine mystery in things. Once you perceive it, you will begin to comprehend it better every day. And you will come at last to love the whole world with an all-embracing love.[1]

God also showed me that the roots of spiritual abuse and sexual scandal and lust are never love. When we stumble, we stumble not over love but over some other idol we've set up in our hearts. (Steve Holsinger of Anchorage, Alaska taught me this.) And we will never remove those idols or protect ourselves from them by denying love or applying the law. Those idols only fall as the true love of God and neighbor displaces them.

Vae Eli, a Samoan chief who has worked with YWAM (Youth With a Mission) for years, told me about his personal

---

[1] Richard Rohr, *Everything Belongs* (New York, NY: The Cross Road Publishing Co., 2003), 28.

journey into love. He shared that in the Samoan culture, boys grow up with a general lack of physical affection, which results in two areas of dysfunction among many Samoan men: lust and violence. When he first came to YWAM, he joined a team that had a whole group of "huggers," which made him feel very uncomfortable. He warned them that being so physical would be problematic for him, and he didn't want to expose them to his own lust problem. He proposed many of the little evangelical rules that we have invented to make affection safe, such as proximity laws or at best, side-hugs. They would have none of it. The ladies in the group all covenanted to keep giving him a

> # Love never fails...
> # and there's no law against it.

big, warm embrace, full of Jesus' love, as a *solution* rather than a *trigger* for any lust that he'd inherited. Sure enough, even knowing his fears, these ladies risked what Vae thought might be defiling, and they hugged the lust right out of him. They proved in practice the words of Scott Evelyn (of Streams Ministries): *Love never fails and there is no law against it.*

This conviction has permeated the heart of our church so thoroughly that we strive to be demonstrative in our love for one another. For example, we've become a hugging church. Led by Andy MacPherson (a staff member who learned "Jesus hugs" from the disabled), we've learned how to offer an embrace in ways that allow for a "no thanks" and can be received without things getting weird. I believe firmly that God's heart for his family includes a culture of affection. As we say often, "Not everyone has the same love language, but everyone needs a hug."

The devil's agenda through various sex and abuse scandals is to make us afraid to show love towards each other; to intimidate us into withdrawing love by inciting paranoia. Pastors and counselors hide behind their desks, physical contact is cold enough to never be mistaken for love, and we protect ourselves with such laws of propriety that we never appear out of bounds. Meanwhile, the incidences of sexual sin in the church actually *increase*. That's NOT a coincidence. When God's love is withheld and Christian affection diminishes, people who are hungry for it will go elsewhere, and then things really *do* get weird.

Meanwhile, Jesus said, "By this shall all men know that ye are my disciples, if ye have love one to another" (John 13: 35 KJV). A question we asked ourselves was, what's happening in our fellowship that an outsider would describe as love? Do we make quick entries and exits on each end of an interesting (or not) staged program? Perhaps the epidemic of church-goers who go home feeling "unfed" has nothing to do with the content of the service. Maybe they just need a little more love. Maybe the consumerist mind-set they bring to church is only partly

---

2 Rowan Williams, *Where God Happens: Discovering Christ in One Another* (Boston: New Seeds, 2005), 24.

the product of our fast-food culture. What if it's a sign that the love-starved aren't finding an embrace at God's table? You will NEVER preach such a person to fullness!

So, as a church, we're taking an honest stab at offering a love that shows. We try to make love tangible by offering words of blessing, the laying on of hands in prayer, and a generous dose of hugs to all who will receive them. We're trying to *become a place where God's love happens.* The miracle is, as it happens through us, it also happens to us. Archbishop of Canterbury Rowan Williams puts it this way:

> Insofar as you open such doors for another, you gain God, in the sense that you become a place where God happens for somebody else. *You become a place where God happens.* God comes to life for somebody else in a life-giving way, not because you are good or wonderful, but because that is what God has done. So, if we can shift our preoccupations, anxiety, and selfishness out of the way to put someone in touch with the possibility of God's healing, to that extent we are ourselves in touch with God's healing. So, if you gain your brother or sister, you gain God.[2]

Rosy

Rosy (not her real name) comes from northern BC, but she makes Fresh Wind her home whenever she is in town. She is poor, struggles with addictions, has experienced a lot of violence, and suffers from the prejudice of being a native Canadian. She told us that she can't get to her seat at Fresh Wind without getting past at least five hugs. Of course not! We see Jesus in her!

Unfortunately, not many do. When she first came to us, it was because she had been referred to us by a church that didn't know how to respond to her. She would try to attend worship services, but whenever the worship started, she would begin to have tremors and choke up phlegm. Suspecting it was a spiritual issue, but not prepared to work through it, they sent her to us.

When Rosy sat down for her first worship time with us, I was pleased to see her relax into a deep peace. With eyes closed, she soaked in God's presence throughout the entire worship set as if she was lazing in a hot tub. On the final song, which happened to be *Amazing Grace*, the action started. She started to tremble and have difficulty breathing. Silently, three intercessors surrounded her, held her, and prayed quietly for peace and freedom. Simultaneously, Eddie (the same Eddie from an earlier chapter) wobbled his way to a microphone and began singing with the team at the top of his lungs. I can't say that his voice is beautiful, but it doesn't lack passion! He seemed to be singing the song just for Rosy, whose reactions increased dramatically as Eddie joined in. I can't explain some of the manifestations we saw (they were messy), but I do know this: by the end of the final verse, Rosy was free. More than that, she was loved. We have embraced her—literally and figuratively—with open arms.

• • • • • •

The anecdotes in this chapter all suggest the need for open arms and open hearts that embrace the other—including the least of these—both literally in loving hugs and metaphorically as we represent the open arms of God the Father here on earth. As we open our arms to welcome the very least and the most lost, we imitate God in four ways outlined in theologian Miroslav Volf's must-read text on justice and reconciliation, *Exclusion and Embrace.*[3]

1. Open arms are a gesture of reaching for the other. They signal discontent with my self-enclosed identity and suggest desire for the other.

2. Open arms say that I have created space in myself for the other to come in. No longer "full of myself," I set out on a journey toward the other, moving beyond my own fortified boundaries.

3. Open arms suggest a fissure in myself—an open door into my space through which the other might enter. They signify an aperture in the boundary of my self.

4. Open arms are a gesture of invitation, like an open door to an expected friend that beckons, come in. But unlike the open door, open arms are also a soft knock on the other's door, politely asking if I might enter their space.

As we open our arms to the world, and especially to the least among us, we proclaim the message of reconciliation—the open temple, the open table, the open arms, the open heart—limited only by what we offer, i.e. the extravagant love of Jesus. To those who respond, to those we receive, we become the Bethlehem innkeeper who might have made room for Christ and his family. If only we have eyes wet enough to see.

---

[3] Miroslav Volf, *Exclusion and Embrace* (Nashville: Abingdon Press, 1996), 141–142.

Soren Kierkegaard
The Invitation - II [4]

Come here all, all, all of you, with Him is rest, and He makes no difficulties, He does but one thing, He opens His arms. He will not first (as righteous people do, alas, even when they are willing to help)—He will not first ask thee, "Art thou not after all to blame for thy misfortune? Hast thou in fact no cause for self-reproach?" It is so easy, so human, to judge after the outward appearance, after the result—when a person is a cripple, or deformed, or has an unprepossessing appearance, to judge that ergo he is a bad man; when a person fares badly in the world so that he is brought to ruin or goes downhill, then to judge that ergo he is a vicious man. Oh, it is such an exquisite invention of cruel pleasure to enhance the consciousness of one's own righteousness in contrast with a sufferer, by explaining that his suffering is God's condign punishment, so that one hardly even... dares to help him; or by challenging him with that condemning question which flatters one's own righteousness in the very act of helping him.

But He will put no such questions to thee, He will not be thy benefactor in so cruel a fashion. If thou thyself art conscious of being a sinner, He will not inquire of thee about it, the bruised reed He will not further break, but He will raise thee up if thou wilt attach thyself to Him. He will not single thee out by contrast, holding thee apart from Him, so that thy sin will seem still more dreadful; He will grant thee a hiding-

---

[4] Soren Kierkegaard, *Training in Christianity* (accessed 29 Mar. 2006) available at http://www.scripturestudies.com/Vol3/C2/c2_cla.html.

place within Him, and once hidden in Him He will hide thy sins. For He is the friend of sinners: When it is a question of a sinner He does not merely stand still, open His arms and say, "Come here"; no, He stands there and waits, as the father of the lost son waited, rather He does not stand and wait, He goes forth to seek, as the shepherd sought the lost sheep, as the woman sought the lost coin. He goes—yet no, He has gone, but infinitely farther than any shepherd or any woman, He went, in sooth, the infinitely long way from being God to becoming man, and that way He went in search of sinners.

Part 5
Following Jesus
on the Narrow Path

·

23

Narrow Door,
Narrow Way

By Brad Jersak

The Word became flesh and blood, and moved into the
neighborhood.

John 1:14 (MSG)

WITH ALL THIS TALK of openness—open temple, open
table, open arms, open hearts—we need to ask ourselves,
"What about the narrow door that Jesus spoke about? Surely, the
message mustn't be so watered down with inclusivism that anything goes! What about the cost of discipleship?"

A fair question. If you haven't asked it by now, I hope you
will. Remember the words of Jesus:

> Enter through the narrow gate. For wide is the gate and broad
> is the road that leads to destruction, and many enter through
> it. But small is the gate and narrow the road that leads to life,
> and only a few find it. (Matthew 7:13–14 NIV)

Historically, the trouble is that religious institutions and their leaders have taken it upon themselves to regulate where the narrow door should be placed and to whom it must be barred. Jesus' rebuke echoes through the centuries:

> Woe to you, teachers of the law and Pharisees, you hypocrites! You shut the kingdom of heaven in men's faces. You yourselves do not enter, nor will you let those enter who are trying to. (Matthew 23:13 NIV)

It's no different in our era. From the ushers who prevented Gandhi from entering the South African church where he would have heard the good news through evangelist Andrew Murray to those in our city who have been instructed to turn away the disabled because they are "too disruptive," Jesus still has a word of woe. It is not for us to create a turnstile where Jesus has installed a very large, permanently open door. The church must relinquish control of the door altogether and get back to the task of issuing invitations in the byways and behind the hedges as per Jesus' instructions. (Scary when you think of who lives in those places—but only until you get to know and love them.)

Christ alone determines the nature of the narrow door. He defined it entirely with two words: "Follow me," by which he seemed to mean "Love your neighbor." The invitation to the throne of grace, the banquet of God, and the arms of Christ is wide open to everyone. But having come and heard his words of life and tasted of his goodness and mercy, we see the Lord rise from the table with a purpose. Those who have said *"Yes"* to this point in the journey are faced with another invitation: the call to follow him in life-offering, risky love. Perhaps it's only the scarcity of takers that have made it a narrow door. Or maybe it seems too difficult. It's warm in the temple; the food at the table is delicious. We like the Jesus on whose bosom we lean. But now where is he going? Maybe we have a premonition that he's off to Gethsemane again, and Golgotha not long after that. Maybe we see him beckoning us to bring our own cross along.

Nice metaphor, but what does it mean? It means that Jesus is inviting us to follow him in his mission where the "Word becomes flesh and moves into the neighborhood." (John 1:14)

This is the secret of the universe: a soon-to-be refugee baby lying in cattle's straw in a poor village in an occupied territory! God becoming one of the least of these. The Word becomes flesh, the message becomes alive, and the gospel becomes love. And now he says, "Follow me. Mimic my love. Take up my mission." It means that it's high time for our message to move from words and sermons and teachings and conferences to become real acts of God's love and life in this world. The Church, like its Lord, must become human.

If Christianity has any relevance in the twenty-first century, it will be because it graduates from hearing what Jesus says to living as he says. This is what it is to be "the wise man who builds his house upon a rock." (Matthew 7:24–27) If our spirituality means anything, it will engender a true conversion that gets us actually living like the One who spent his life rescuing the world. In other words, like Christ, we are to be an incarnational message of God's love, especially to the least of these that he calls his little brothers and sisters. This narrow way is marked by the Cross, because God's love requires at least two kinds of death:

1. We need to die to our contempt, which is a kind of subtle "looking down" hatred of *"the other."* The most obvious *others* are those with whom we wage war, whether in faraway places with people of other religions, politics, and pigment or those we battle nearby in the culture wars over sexuality, morality, and so on. If the way we respond to "worldly sin issues" is full of *contempt, rejection,* and *exclusion,* then our ways are just as much "works of the flesh" as anything we're opposing (Galatians 5: 19–20 lumps them together). We need to bring those ways to the Cross and put them to death or *we simply have not followed Christ and wandered off the narrow path of love.*

2. Second, Christ calls us to follow him to the Cross of "co-suffering love." We enter into the mystery of suffering *with* people and then look around for God. It means saying, "Yes, I am willing," when God's heart breaks open your heart and then expands it to accommodate a world-sized vision. During prayer, my friend Heidi Miller saw this as a globe wearing pregnancy pants! Something's about to "pop" in this earth, and God is looking for midwives. The thing is, what if God's plan through Christ really is to save the world? What if the flesh Christ is now wearing in this neighborhood is us? And what if saving the world is no more grandiose than serving the least person that we know? Will we follow?

As the Lord leaves the banqueting table and heads out the narrow door (see, it's wide door *in*, narrow door *out*), he looks over his shoulder, hears your unspoken questions, and answers, "Sure, come along... [sober pause] *but come along."*

Frances Ridley Havergal
"Going Forth With the King"[1]

'The King said, Wherefore wentest thou not with me?'

'With me!' To be with our King will be our highest bliss for eternity; and surely it is the position of highest honour and gladness now. But if we would always *be* with Him, we must sometimes be ready to *go* with Him.

'The Son of God goes forth to war' now-a-days. Do we go with Him? His cross is 'without the gate.' Do we go 'forth unto Him without the camp bearing His reproach'? Do we really go with Him every day and all day long, following 'the Lamb whithersoever He goeth'? What about this week—this day? Have we loyally gone with our King wherever His banner, His footsteps go before?

If the voice of our King is heard in our hearts, 'Where wentest *thou* not with me?'—thou who hast eaten 'continually at the King's table,'—thou who hast had a place among 'the King's sons,'—thou unto whom the King has shown 'the kindness of God,' we have no 'because' to offer. He would have healed the spiritual lameness that hindered, and we might have run after Him. We are without excuse. It is only now that we can go with Jesus into conflict, suffering,

---

[1] Frances Ridley Havergal, *My King or Daily Thoughts for the King's Children* (London: James Nisbet and Co., 1870), 37-39.

loneliness, weariness. It is only now that we can come to the help of the Lord against the mighty in this great battlefield. Shall we shrink from opportunities which are not given to the angels? Surely, even with Him in glory, the disciples must 'remember the words of the Lord Jesus, how He said,' to them, 'Ye are they which have continued *with me* in my temptations,' with a thrill of rapturous thanksgiving that such a privilege was theirs.

There will be no more suffering with Him in heaven, only reigning with Him; no more fighting under His banner, only sitting with Him on His throne. But to-day we may prove our loving and grateful allegiance to our King in the presence of His enemies, by rising up and going forth with Him, forth *from* a life of easy idleness or selfish business,—forth *into* whatever form of blessed fellowship in His work, His wars, or, may be, of His sufferings, the King Himself may choose for us. We have heard His call, 'Come *unto* me,' To-day He says, 'Come *with* me.'

24

Acid Test: Interviews from Burma

By Brad Jersak

What an honor to think that all of you before me are Christ!
Even the humblest peasant, who may be pondering there
next to a radio, you are Christ! For your baptism is one with
the death and resurrection of the Lord.

Oscar Romero

In January 2006, I went on a pilgrimage to Thailand with a
specific agenda: to visit the Karen people, an ethnic minor-
ity from the Karen state in Burma.[1] These precious people live
under extreme persecution that would make Hitler blush with
either pride or shame. The Burmese military and their puppet

---

[1] In solidarity with the Karen people, I do not acknowledge the military
junta's renaming of Burma.

militia groups continue to raze their villages, gang rape and torture women and children, plant minefields, destroy harvests, and abduct people for forced labour. They use amputation as just one of their weapons of terror. Today, two million internally displaced persons live inside of Burma, with up to 70,000 child soldiers now roaming the jungles. Add to that tens of thousands living in refugee camps on the Thai side of the river for several generations, and you've got a recipe for hell on earth.

I had the privilege of visiting Karen refugee camps (of up to 50,000 people) and villages on both the Thai and Burmese side of the border. The community in Burma had previously been burnt to the ground four times in two other locations. My hope was that I could hear about the narrow path of Jesus from the Karen people and from those who are helping them. My sense was that these people could provide an acid test for that which I've been hearing, seeing, and writing about the narrow way. In other words, if it didn't make sense in their situation, it probably wouldn't make sense anywhere. If it's not true there—if it can't be lived out in the refugee camps or in the aftermath of a village-burning—then maybe it's not true at all. Much of what passes for western spirituality is proven to be no more than fluff in such a context, so what better place to test my thesis?

Interview 1: The Family of the White Monkey

My first interview was with an American whose family has given their lives to the narrow path of risky love. Believe me, that's an understatement. They are known as "the family of the white monkey," nicknamed after their oldest daughter (about five-years-old), who was so-named for her endless energy. As it turns out, an old Karen legend prophesied, "When the people are oppressed, a white monkey will come to help you." And so it has. This little girl, along with her two younger siblings (one is still nursing) and her radical parents, are part of an NGO called the "Free Burma Rangers" (www.freeburmarangers.org).

FBR trains and leads teams of Karen nationals throughout the jungles of Burma, where they find and gather people who have been driven out of their burned villages, guide them between battalions of Burmese soldiers through the minefields and mortar fire and into hiding places. There, they give them emergency first-aid for injuries, medicine, blankets, and clothes. They also document human rights abuses. Most important of all, they deliver much needed love on the heels of the horrendous atrocities these people have suffered. Their motto is:

Love each other. Unite and work for freedom, justice, and peace. Forgive and don't hate each other. Pray with faith, act with courage, never surrender.

After seeing photos of this family traipsing through the jungle with three children in tow, I was able to chat with "the mother of the white monkey" about her version of the narrow path of Jesus' high-risk love. Here's how it went:

Brad: It seems to me that your family is following what Jesus called the narrow way—the way of risky love. Tell me about that kind of life.

Mom: I believe in John 10:10 where Jesus says that he came to give us the good life—the abundant life. I want that for my children. There is a western version of the abundant life that is all about having and getting—about accumulating and preserving your own life. But we have chosen to take our kids into the jungle to teach them an alternative—another way to live. By the time they are ten years old, we hope that they will really own the abundant life as the Karen people have taught it:

"Mai La"

1. Simplicity: these people live contentedly in a bamboo house, eating deep-fried frogs and fish paste. They have found a way to be joyful and natural.

2. Hospitality: Their attitude is, "Come into my house. Stay as long as you like. You don't need to call ahead, and the host doesn't need to provide extras. Just bring along something that you can share with everyone."

3. Generosity: Their greeting is, "Come eat with me," and they really mean it. The question is not whether we'll eat all their food. It's simply a greeting that expresses their shared generosity.

4. Compassion: This means helping someone's hurt. The FBR students lay down their lives for their people wherever the fighting is.

Brad: What about the danger level and your children's safety. Is that scary for you? Or for them?

Mom: First, we do what we can to settle the kids into a stable (not necessarily safe) base camp away from the shelling. We try not to scare them, using the movie *Life is Beautiful* as an example. Everyone is treated as uncle or aunt, so the children experience tons of love. We teach them that good and evil are relevant. Some people are evil, but we are here to do the good thing. We don't need to worry, because God opens these doors for us, and we're doing what he's doing.

Second, we live by certain convictions (settled beliefs):

1. These people need our help.

2. I need to be where my deepest desire meets people's deepest needs. We believe in this mission, this work.

3. Most of all, there is great *freedom* in laying down your life rather than stressing out trying to preserve it. There is great *peace* in knowing that there is more to life than the number of days we live here. Fullness of days is more about the quality of our lives than how old we are when we finally die. I'm not sure how close my daughter was to dying of fever and illness on this last trip. But I know that whatever time God gives her is full of abundance—the good life—as he meant it to be.

I believe that if God sends you somewhere or gives you something to do, you should do it until he moves you on. One day when I thought about giving up and going back to the US, I had a vision. I was in the middle of a lake, and it felt like the water had become too deep. I was treading water, but I was scared. I decided to swim for the bank to have a rest, but when I got to the bank, I saw Jesus was still out in the middle of the lake. He was holding his arms out and saying, "I am here with you." I decided then that it was better to be with Jesus in the middle of the lake than to be on my own on the bank.

Interview 2: Steve Gumaer of Partners

Steve and Oddney Gumaer are the founders and directors of *Partners* (www.partnersworld.org), a grassroots relief and development agency that works with the Karen people and other ethnic minorities in Burma along four lines:

1. Medical relief

2. Educational development

3. Crisis relief

4. Capacity building (enriching people's skills by training medics, teachers, etc.)

In Steve, I saw someone who practiced Proverbs 31:8–9:

Speak up for the people who have no voice,
for the rights of all the down-and-outers.
Speak out for justice!
Stand up for the poor and destitute!

I felt that he could share the ways which he has seen these people walk the narrow way. Here's what he said:

We've started working with another people group in Burma called the *Karenni*. Like the Karen, they have been targeted by the Burmese government for eradication. In the last ten years, 2,500 of their villages have been burned to the ground.

Partners supplies medicine for the poor and sick, and money towards developing schools in their villages. For example, there are seven villages with 2,000 children who need education. *Partners'* vision is to build a school for each of those villages.

But just yesterday, my friend from FBR called me on the satellite phone from one of those villages. He said, "Listen to this!" I could hear mortar fire and guns in the background. I could hear that my friends were being shot at. He reported that all seven villages had just been burned, people had been selectively killed, women were gang-raped, then their breasts had been amputated and burned, some of this their children were forced to watch.

FBR had arrived to find a lone medic working on an elderly man. The man had returned to his burned down home and was digging for any remaining possessions when a landmine blew his leg off. The medic was performing a life-saving amputation with a Leatherman™ knife—his seventh such operation that day.

But these people are resistant. They say, "We'll flee, but we will not leave." They wait in the jungle, then re-emerge to rebuild. Those Karenni are all Christian. When the villages were burned, somehow one of the churches survived. They had seven church services throughout the day to accommodate all the believers.

This morning, my friend called on the satellite phone again. And again he said, "Listen to this!" In the background, I could hear the Karenni people, now standing in the ashes of their village as medical supplies from *Partners* arrived. They were singing old Baptist praise hymns in four-part harmony!

I made a decision in my heart. I can no longer treat these people as statistics or refugees. They are my neighbors. What does this mean? It means that I cannot treat them as objects or numbers to be served. I cannot simply say "What would Jesus do?" in some vague way. I let my heart care for them as I would my own children. It means I must let them into my heart. The image of God in me must see the image of God in them and act as I would for my own family. If the house is burning down and I hear my children crying out from inside, I don't stop to ask, "Is this safe? Is this legal? Is this appropriate?" I rush in and save the children, even if it means giving my life.

So, what is the Karenni's version of the narrow way? Their lives and faith have gone through the acid test of persecution. Where do we find them? Standing in the ashes rejoicing.

You see, there is a part of their souls that cannot be touched. No one can take away the part of life that God gives, even if they are killed. That sacred part of their hearts is free—freer even than their oppressors.

Interview 3: Pu Ton: A Real Apostle

It's one thing to hear from those who are giving their lives to work with the IDP's (Internally Displaced Persons) and refugees. It was a whole new world actually hearing from the Karen people firsthand. I met Pu (Grandpa) Ton in the Mae-La camp where I enjoyed the hospitality and generosity that I had heard about. I was treated to a fine meal of delicious, spicy Karen food in a simple thatched bamboo hut that sat on stilts. Pu Ton is seventy-five. For over forty years, he acted as a missionary church-planter to the Wa people. He would lead apostolic teams to engage in holistic ministry that included:

1. Preaching the good news

2. Education – from primary school to Bible school

3. Environmental education

4. Agriculture/Husbandry

5. Health care

They were able to co-exist peacefully with the Buddhists and animists, who would often convert to Christianity simply because they saw the love and peace of God in the face of both superstition and persecution. Now, for over a decade, he has been removed to a refugee camp where he continues to support the

Bible school and churches that have sprung up from the clay. He was a man of fairly few words, but tremendous authority. When I asked him about the narrow way, he said:

> The key to revival is martyrdom. Martyrdom is a sturdy foundation for the church. We have experienced persecution, but we are also witnesses that blessing follows persecution. So we thank God for it. We thank him, because that is when we see how much God loves us. For every martyr, a thousand more come to know the love of God.
>
> Through this persecution, we have learned the power of prayer. We have learned the power of forgiveness. We have learned how to bless the very enemies who killed our families. And we see our enemies change. This is the message of the gospel. The Cross leads to peace and reconciliation.

Conclusion

During my brief tour of Thailand, I can honestly say that I did not *learn* the narrow way of Jesus' risky love. But I did *hear* about it, I witnessed it, and what I saw may become a foundation for learning it. To say, "Yes, I will follow," is only the first step and, having seen a little of where it can lead, I suspect that my "Yes" is tainted by some of the good intentions I see at the end of Luke 9 or the fickleness of Peter before he denied the Lord three times. Some of the people I met didn't get to choose their crown of thorns. It was thrust on them by where and when they were born. Others picked up their cross willingly and moved into the thicket of Burmese war zones because Christ's love compelled them. But what about me? What does "follow me" look like in my life? I'm still pursuing that question in prayer.

Nevertheless, I saw Jesus in those folks. I watched them open wide their super-long, knee-high tables to all who were hungry and thirsty. And I met Jesus in them, challenging me to rise from the table and follow him into the narrow way of co-suffering love. I felt Jesus in them when they laid hands on me in prayer or outgave me with love-gifts. I heard Jesus in them, quietly sharing their stories yet finding a way to smile and laugh at the conclusion. I leave you these final thoughts from my journal.

* * * * * *

The way of Jesus is the way of Jesus' love. It's the only way. 1 Corinthians 13 says that apart from love—tongues, prophecies, miracles, and even martyrdom are utterly worthless. The only thing that matters is faith expressing itself in love (Galatians 5:6). Faith Godward, love manward is the way prescribed by Christ for his disciples, indeed, for all humanity.

He blazed this path, the way of sacrificial, serving love and I suspect that there are many who've found that path even while still looking for the One who forged it. Once on it, they will surely begin to sense his fragrance, even in their fellow travellers, and will ultimately, inevitably catch up to him. This is important, for locating the One who cuts this trail through the jungle of history enables us to stay on the Way.[2]

---

[2] Cf. Andrew Klager, "The Centrality of Christ as Participation," *Clarion Journal of Spirituality and Justice,* Vol. 6, Mar. 2006 (Lent) 29-33.

The saving work of Christ, the "new Adam," is far more dramatic, powerful, and effective than the fall of the first Adam. He has secured something in this world by his sacrifice that extends to all. Now he is asking, not simply, "Are you saved, brother?" but "Who will be my apprentices in this world? My grace extends beyond what you know, so rejoice. But now, who will follow me? Who will participate in my kingdom agenda? Will you let me teach you how to 'do' this life?"

I also suspect that many who profess Christ have departed radically from the narrow path. They follow ways in his name that meander towards destruction or set their own highway that leads multitudes away from the way of Christ, which is the love of God, brother, neighbor, and enemy.

Faith includes trusting that Jesus' way is the way to life, even though it surely looks like death. The high road takes us through some low places. It's not for nothing that it's called both the way of life AND the way of the Cross.

What matters is that *the least of these* line the road.

Find them, love them, serve them, and the narrow way is not far off. The poor, the meek, the mourning, the peacemakers, the justice-hungry are those who walk this path. They define the way and take us to the Way, to Jesus. The question at this point is less about whether we or they have said the sinner's prayer and more about *if* and *how* we're oriented to the path that Jesus made. For our part, let's invite the world and the church to courageously walk that path and to proclaim the One who walked it first... the One we see in the least of these.

25

Christ:
My Beloved Enemy

By Brad and Eden Jersak

> You prepare a table before me
> in the presence of my enemies.
> Psalm 23:5 (NIV)

At a recent *Open Temple, Open Table* seminar, a woman said to me, "I had a dream about you last night." Never start a conversation that way. As I held my breath, she continued, "It was very brief. You were just finishing a teaching time by saying, 'Remember. Remember to bless your enemies.'" With a sigh of relief, I replied, "That was a good dream."

The Dogma Of Love

Christian discipleship is Jesus' invitation to follow him on the often narrow way of sacrificial love. The way (i.e. lifestyle) of love was not optional or peripheral to Christ's message. In fact, it comprises the very core of his teaching… so central that we might refer to Jesus' "dogma of love." Conversely, failure to love becomes the great sin and the prime heresy. What distinguished Christ's message, the message of the kingdom, from all others was a simple and absolute commandment to love at all costs, even unto death. He lays it out in no uncertain terms. According to Jesus, to enter the kingdom, you must:

- love God
- love your brother and sister
- love your neighbor
- love your enemy

This final point is "the kicker" because it is the ultimate test-case of faithfulness to Christ. This is both what Christ asked for and precisely what he did. His teaching and his life led to a single destination: the Cross on which he died, praying, "Father, forgive them." Let's recall how Jesus preached his message.

Love Your Enemies

You have heard that it was said, 'Eye for eye, and tooth for tooth.' But I tell you, Do not resist an evil person. If someone strikes you on the right cheek, turn to him the other also. And if someone wants to sue you and take your tunic, let him have your cloak as well. If someone forces you to go one mile, go with him two miles. Give to the one who asks you, and do not turn away from the one who wants to borrow from you.

You have heard that it was said, 'Love your neighbor and hate your enemy.' But I tell you: Love your enemies and pray for those who persecute you, that you may be sons of your Father in heaven. He causes his sun to rise on the evil and the good, and sends rain on the righteous and the unrighteous. If you love those who love you, what reward will you get? Are not even the tax collectors doing that? And if you greet only your brothers, what are you doing more than others? Do not even pagans do that? Be perfect, therefore, as your heavenly Father is perfect. (Matthew 5:38-48 NIV)

Throughout the epistle of 1 John, the apostle identifies love of brother and neighbor as the measure by which I actually know God and have eternal life! If I claim to love God, but in fact hate my [immediate or global] neighbor, John calls me a liar. The apostle Paul maintains that even under threat of death, we must follow the example of Christ in rejecting vengeance (Matt. 26:52-53, Rom. 12:17-21) and going like sheep to the slaughter (Isa. 53:7, Rom. 8:36) because even death is no threat to God's love.

My Enemy as the Least of These

I bring up love for one's enemy in the context of seeing Jesus in the least of these because for me, I truly treat my enemies as "the least favored" in my heart. I exclude them as "the other" and marginalize them from my sphere of love. I have a least favorite brother in my church, a least favorite neighbor on my cul-de-sac, and a MOST favorite enemy at large in the world. Really! I refuse to live in denial of my contempt, my propensity to hate, because only by naming them as "enemies" honestly in my heart can I finally hear Christ's command (yes, command!) to love and bless and pray for them. Why does he require this of me? Of course there is the biblical response, "So that I will be like my Father in heaven" who loved me and sent his Son to die for me while I was still his enemy (Rom. 5:10). But I believe there is more to it than that. Could it be that our enemies are servants of God, prescribed to save us, to heal us, and to sculpt us into the image of Christ?

My Enemy as a Servant of Christ

Graham Cooke, a prophetic minister from the UK, once suggested this in a story he told of two "enemies" who followed him from town to town opposing his ministry. They would track his conference schedule and send pamphlets ahead to churches in the cities where he would be speaking, warning them that Graham was a false prophet and describing the errors he was allegedly making. They would show up at his meetings, sitting in the front row and taking scrupulous notes in an effort to gather further "ammo" against him. These self-appointed watchdogs of Christian orthodoxy represented a real thorn in Graham's side.

As I heard him tell the story, Graham described a dream that changed his whole perspective. He saw himself sitting with the Lord on his throne (Eph. 2:6) and a block of precious stone was brought before them. He then saw some hands carefully sculpting the marble block into a beautiful statue. Curious and impatient, Graham asked the Lord how they might speed up the process. The Lord replied, "It will go more quickly if you encourage them." Sure enough, as Graham began to bless the sculptors, their work accelerated and intensified. Soon, he was standing on the armrest of the throne and cheering the craftsmen on. Meanwhile, angels were laying around the throne, holding their bellies in riotous laughter. When the statue was finished, Graham saw that it was an image of himself, patterned perfectly after the image of Christ. He wept at its beauty. So what did the angels find so funny? It was the fact that Graham was cheering on and blessing the very men who had been stalking him and making his life miserable. Neither they nor Graham were aware until that moment that they were God's servants, forming his character into something beautiful and Christ-like… *if Graham would bless them.* When Graham exchanged his frustration for a true blessing, the men *immediately* abandoned their mission!

Indebted to Our Debtors

Teresa of Avila, discussing in the Lord's Prayer, comes to the phrase, "Lord, forgive us our debts, even as we forgive our debtors." She exhorts us to rejoice in involuntary trials (persecution by our enemies) since they are exceedingly more efficient than voluntary trials (fasting, asceticism) in our spiritual progress. Speaking of the perfected soul, she says:

> [Unless] a person is very resolute, and makes a point, if the occasion arises, of forgiving, not only these mere nothings which people call wrongs, but any wrong, however grave, you need not think much of that person's prayer. For wrongs have no effect upon a soul whom God draws to Himself in such sublime prayer as this, nor does it care if it is highly esteemed or not… having already discovered by experience what great benefits the soul gains and what progress it makes when it suffers for God's sake. For only very rarely does His

Majesty grant it such great consolations, and then only to those who have willingly borne many trials for His sake. For contemplatives have to bear heavy trials, and therefore the Lord seeks out for Himself souls of great experience.

A great wrong, or a great trial, may cause them some momentary distress, but they will hardly have felt it when reason will intervene, and will seem to raise its standard aloft, and drive away their distress by giving them the joy of seeing how God has entrusted them with the opportunity of gaining, in a single day, more lasting favours and graces in His Majesty's sight than they could gain in ten years by means of trials which they sought on their own account.[1]

Gollum's Role

I was very glad to hear these warnings when I did, because they "re-storied" my trials as a youth-worker through the 1990's. The teenagers in my youth group were passionate in their pursuit of genuine Christianity. My senior pastor gave us a lot of space to make mistakes that led ultimately to growth and fruitfulness. I was not one to play it safe, often walking the fine line between folly and the so-called "cutting edge." In any case, as you can imagine, not everyone in that established church had patience for things avant-garde. Over the course of a decade, I developed a "beloved enemy" who seemed annoyed by nearly every idea I presented or decision I made. He would frequently attempt to block me at the leadership level. When he succeeded, I was upset. When he

---

[1] Teresa of Avila, *The Way of Perfection,* trans. and ed. by E. Allison Peers, 1964 (accessed 11 Mar. 2006) available at http://www.franciscansfo.org/Avila/WofP7.htm#36.

failed, he was upset. Our disagreements were occasionally heated and our behavior threatened to divide the leadership and even the church. I doubt that God took much pleasure in this. Finally, when we clashed over the tenure of our pastor, things came to a head. A mutual confidante shared that "hate" was not too strong a term for my nemesis' feelings towards me. For my part, I accused him before the Lord of being a "Judas." It was only by God's mercy that we weren't both disqualified from the Lord's service.

In preparation for a mediated reconciliation meeting, the Lord called me to see this elder with the eyes of Jesus. I gave it a try. I expected God to reveal some hidden nobility in the man that would arouse my respect… or perhaps some aspect of brokenness that would incite compassion. I was in for a surprise. At the Cross in prayer, what I saw was *Gollum,* a character from J.R.R. Tolkien's *Lord of the Rings!* This ghoulish vision of my enemy was at once pathetic and repulsive. I don't believe the Lord saw my enemy this way… No, God was showing me how *I* had judged this fellow. He also revealed that the barely-repressed hatred in my heart functioned like a curse—a death-sentence— on this man who was also my brother (Matt. 5:21-22). With the vision came a reminder—a speech from Tolkien's *Fellowship of the Ring*: the wizard Gandalf's prophetic warning to Frodo when he had wished Gollum dead:

> Deserves [death]? I dare say he does. Many that live deserve death. And some that die deserve life. Can you give it to them? Then do not be too eager to deal out death in judgement. For even the very wise cannot see all ends. I have

not much hope that Gollum can be cured before he dies, but
there is a chance of it. And he is bound up with the fate of the
Ring. My heart tells me that he has some part to play yet, for
good or ill, before the end; and when that comes, the pity of
Bilbo may rule the fate of many—yours not least.[2]

The message I received from Graham Cooke, Teresa of
Avila, and J.R.R. Tolkien was that God's call to be merciful, to
bless, and even to LOVE my enemy was not only for his sake,
but for mine as well. My character and destiny were inexorably
wrapped up in his. My response to him would either hinder or
hasten God's plan to fashion me into the man he created me to
be. In retrospect, I can see that this is exactly what happened.
No one can take more credit for my personal growth during that
period than my beloved enemy. Looking back, I now see Christ's
handiwork through the one I once despised. I wished that I could
thank him without seeming facetious, but happily, he knows it
now from the vantage point of heaven. He is now part of my
cloud of witnesses. God's eternal blessings to you, sir.

This is not to justify the sins of our enemies or to deny the
hurt they've caused. Yet, I don't merely bless them in spite of
their maltreatment. I see their place in God's great redemptive
purposes for my life. When I love and bless my enemies, I am
living the narrow path of Jesus' love. When I forgive them and
pray for them, God even begins to heal me of the wounds they
had inflicted.

---

[2] J.R.R. Tolkien, *Lord of the Rings: The Fellowship of the Ring* (London:
George Allen and Unwin Ltd., 1966) 69.

However, if I balk and resort to dehumanizing my enemy, I only diminish myself. For example, let's move from the personal scale to the global scene. If I see the foreign militant as an animal worthy of slaughter, I will give myself or my government permission to treat them as such, thus reducing myself to the role of either butcher or predator. If I ignore God's command to leave vengeance to him, or if I neglect to walk the path of peacemaking (overcoming evil with good), I will allow myself to indulge in cruelty to the cruel. I may entertain the possibility and finally the necessity of "soft torture" in the service of the greater good. Eventually, I may even attribute such crusades to God's will.

Is this scenario not a renewed betrayal of the Prince of Peace? Who are the sons and daughters of the kingdom but the peacemakers, forgivers, and reconcilers? To abandon this path of God's love seems to me a way laying the Cross back down and rejecting the Way of Life. It begins when I cease to see Jesus in the least of these—in this case, Jesus in my enemy.

As my family has grappled with love and hate in a culture stripped of grace (as Miroslav Volf calls it), we've seen the importance of coming back to "the table prepared for me in the presence of my enemies" (Psalm 23). We ask ourselves, "Who are my enemies? Why are they at the table? When am I the enemy?" I close this chapter with a meditation by my wife, Eden, who has been engaging with these questions. What has the Lord said to her? How did she respond?

* * * * * *

In the Presence of Mine Enemies

He is wooing you from the jaws of distress
to a spacious place free from restriction,
to the comfort of your table laden with choice food.

Job 36:16 (NIV)

I find myself in the jaws of distress once again. But then I hear God calling me, wooing me. I turn from my distress and follow the Good Shepherd back to the wide-open spaces of safety. There, in the midst of freedom, is the table. I sit down, still stinging from the wounds the jaws of distress have inflicted, and survey the table. All those same wonderful things are still in abundance on the table, only I've lost my appetite in the midst of what I've just gone through. So while the blessings on this table are exactly what I need, I'm not able to partake. I can't seem to consume the very things I need the most. Then I look up from the table and see my enemy standing before me (Psalm 23:5). When I used to read this passage, I imagined the devil standing there, and so it was easy to sit and eat when he was someone I equated only with pain. It was easy to sit smugly and enjoy my feast when the enemy present was an "evil-doer." But more recently, I have begun to put a name and face to that enemy. It's no longer some red-faced, horned, fork-tailed creature, but a living, breathing person (and often someone I love). Now that person stands watching me at this banquet, and I'm to enjoy this table in this person's presence?

Love your enemies. Bless those that curse you.

I have a lot of questions. I was wooed here to this table, and my enemy is present and seems to be here with permission. Was my enemy invited to this table as well? How am

I supposed to eat in front of this person? Why am I being honored with lavish blessings in this person's presence? Why is it so much harder to receive with my enemy standing before me? Now that my enemy has a name and a face, everything changes. A real person stands in place of the enemy, and yet I know that this person loves both God and me. This doesn't make sense. The enemy is supposed to be someone who hates me, not someone who loves me!

Love your enemies. Bless those that curse you.

The foundation I stand on is beginning to shake, and I begin to feel unsure of myself. A bigger question creeps into my mind, and I'm not sure I want to know the answer. If someone I love and who loves God can stand at my table in the place of my enemy, at whose table do I stand in the place of the enemy? Is that possible? Would I be considered the enemy in anyone else's life—not in an evil, devilish sort of way, but as someone who is able to wound those around her? If so, where does that lead?

Love your enemies. Bless those that curse you.

Why has this table been prepared for me in the presence of my enemy? I'm convinced this isn't some cruel joke on God's behalf, so then what is the point? Why would the jaws of distress be invited to my safe place? I was just rescued from that very thing. What is God up to?

Love your enemies. Bless those that curse you.

I look back down and consider the blessings God has prepared for me on this table. My questions stop for the moment, and I focus on the Good Shepherd beside me. I see compassion flowing out of his eyes; compassion for me, the one he has rescued out of his delight for me (2 Samuel 22:20). I see love that overlooks my foolishness at being caught in those jaws again. I see mercy for any other role I may take at anyone else's table. And I see grace for me, that I may be invited to this table and given this wonderful banquet of blessings without any sort of merit on my part.

Love your enemies. Bless those that curse you.

Then a thought dawns on me, and I am horrified by what it suggests. How often have I been the enemy at God's table? How often have I stood there in contempt and watched him partake?

I can handle the reality of being at some other persons table as the enemy, but at God's own table? Shame and deep grief rise up in me, and I want to flee from this place. I want to run away and not let this truth be seen by my enemy. But then we look at each other, my beloved enemy and I, I see that same shame and grief. We mirror each other's hearts. Then yet another question hits me:

What if I am the enemy at my own table?

Love your enemies. Bless those that curse you.

It is true. I have sat in both seats at this wonderful banquet of blessings. He has invited me twice. He wanted to make sure that I would be there, that I would be blessed. Can I love this enemy? Can I bless this enemy? Can I share compassion and mercy, grace and love? Can I invite this enemy to my table? Can I invite my beloved enemy to sit at this table to be blessed? Can I bless the one who has cursed me and love the one who has hated me? My questions await an answer... a final word.

Love your enemies. Bless those that curse you.

26

The Beatitudes:
Map for the Narrow Path

By Ron Dart[1]

Ron Dart is a spiritual father who has led me on many a hike up the narrow paths of the Cascade Mountains in Northern Washington. On these walks, he has also called me to move further up and further into God's kingdom. The Beatitudes of Jesus are his key map. On this count, I defer to my mentor.

Seeing the crowds, Jesus went up on the mountain, and when he sat down, his disciples came to him. And he opened his mouth and taught them.

"The Divine Life is for those who die to the demands of the ego. Such people will inhabit the Kingdom of Heaven.

---

[1] This essay originally appeared as Ron Dart, "Justice and Spirituality: The Vision of the Beatitudes," *Clarion Journal of Spirituality and Justice*, July 2004 (accessed 3 Mar. 2006) available at http://www.clarion-journal.ca/article.php?story=20040721070219326. Used by permission.

The Divine Life is for those who have lived through tragedy and suffering. Such people will be comforted at a deep level.

The Divine Life is for those who bring their passions under control for goodness. It is such people that will inherit the earth.

The Divine Life is for those who hunger and thirst for justice. Such people will be fed to the full.

The Divine Life is offered to those who are gracious and merciful. Such people will be treated in a merciful and gracious manner.

The Divine Life is offered to those whose Home is clean on the inside. Such people will know the very presence of God and see his face.

The Divine Life is offered to those who are Makers and Creators of Peace. Such people will be called the children of God.

The Divine Life is known by those who are persecuted for seeking Justice. Such people will know what it means to live in the Kingdom of Heaven.

The Divine Life is known by those who are mistreated and misunderstood in their passion for justice. They will inherit the Kingdom of Heaven. The prophets were treated this way in the past."

Matthew 5:1-12 (Ron Dart)[2]

---

[2] Translation by Ron Dart. Cf. Ron Dart, *The Beatitudes: When Mountain Meets Valley* (Abbotsford, BC: Fresh Wind Press, 2005).

I concentrated on the Sermon on the Mount. It was startling to me that I could not recall a sermon ever preached on this manifesto of Christ's new social order in my church when I was growing up. I vaguely remembered some talk about the Sermon on the Mount not being applicable to our time, that it was meant for the time when we all would get to heaven. The Sermon revealed to me what Jesus meant by the Kingdom of God. In it, Jesus calls those who follow him to a life that completely undermines the values and structures of this world and opens up possibilities of a new one. The way of life described in the Sermon is truly revolutionary, much deeper and more radical than the revolutionary movements of which had had a taste. The way of Jesus overturns the assumptions of Right, Left, and Middle, and presents a genuinely new option for both our personal and political lives. It calls for a life lived for God, for neighbor, for the poor, and even for enemies.[3]

Jim Wallis

The Cry for Justice

There is an abiding interest in spirituality these days, but when the interest in spirituality does not lead to a passion for justice, it becomes a veiled and subtle form of narcissism. There is a hunger for justice in our time, but when the longing for justice is not shaped by a historically informed spirituality,

---

[3] Jim Wallis, *Revive Us Again: A Sojourner's Story* (Nashville, TN: Abingdon Press,1983) 74.

the passion for justice can become a brittle form of ideology. The Beatitudes, when rightly read and wisely internalized, offer us a way and means of growing in inner integrity and living forth our faith in a just and peacemaking manner.

The Beatitudes begin with a call to leave the many demands of life in the valley and ascend the peaks to hear a deeper word, a fuller word. We are called to be poor of spirit, to turn inward and see those things we are to let go of, those things we cling to that must be released. It is only as we are empty that we can be filled. We are, in fact, asked to come and die, to allow the small seed of the ego to dissolve and disappear, to break through its constricting skin, so a fuller, a richer, a resurrected life will emerge. The more we allow ourselves to be emptied of our agendas and inadequate notions of identity, the more we will be filled with a sense of our kinship and solidarity with others, but we will also become more acutely aware of the gap between what we long to be and what we truly are. As we become aware of our poverty, we come to see the subtle forms that sin can take in our lives. It is in this tension between what we aspire to be and who we know we are that we learn what it means to mourn with those who suffer. The more we allow ourselves to feel such pain the more we seek to do something about it. It is through longing to do something about such suffering and injustice that we are walked into the meaning of meekness. Tragically, meekness has been misinterpreted in much of Christendom. Meekness does not mean passively accepting what is. Meekness means disciplining our passions and bringing them under control for goodness, and the hunger for goodness is about an unquenchable desire to ask questions about why there is suffering.

Looking Inward

The first three Beatitudes, then, are about the transformation of the inner life, and, as such, the necessary issues that must be faced before we step out onto the stage of the outer life. We are invited to be poor, to let go of our ego. As we walk this path, we are offered the gift of a feeling for the injustices and suffering in the world. The more we allow ourselves to be filled with this deeper love, the fullness of God's abundant Grace, the more we open ourselves to allow that love to reshape our identity and reorient our desires toward the good; this is the meaning of meekness. The inner life, now prepared and properly attired, is ready to enter, in spirit and truth, the outer world.

Looking Outward

Jesus, after walking us from room to room in the interior life, then points the way to the outer life. If we are willing to die to our ego, if we are truly one with the God of Love (which means a God of Justice and Mercy), then we will ask why there is injustice in the world and what can be done about it. Jesus makes it quite clear that the inner life must lead to a hunger and thirst for justice. Unfortunately, we have often translated and interpreted, 'Blessed are those who hunger and thirst for justice' as 'Blessed are those who hunger and thirst for righteousness,' then reduced the meaning of righteousness to personal and private piety. The text will not grant us this sort of indulgence (any more than the prophets of old will). Jesus, in fact, is calling us to be seekers of justice, of the common good. When the deeper vision of this verse becomes reduced to a private and personal desire to live a life of holiness and integrity, we sanitize the text and mute its power and fullness. An interest in spirituality that lacks a hunger and thirst for justice is both an opiate and a diversion.

Justice is about asking why there is poverty, why there is injustice, who are the powerful that perpetuate such evils and what can be done about it. There is, in fact, a moral plumb line by which empires, nations, communities and individuals can be measured, and if we lose this vigorous moral vision, the religious journey can slip into sentimentality. The quest for justice must always be balanced by a concern for mercy. Blessed are those who are merciful. Those who seek justice often ask the hard questions and sacrifice much, but they can, at times, lack mercy, graciousness and charity. Those who only play the strings of mercy often contribute to injustice by their refusal to ask why the poor are poor. Jesus never separated justice and mercy. Neither should we.

Those who have spent much time in the outer world of justice and mercy know only too well the hurt and harm that can come to the heart. Despair and cynicism can come to dominate the day, and dark clouds can circle the soul. This is why Jesus then brings us back to the inner life. Blessed are the pure of heart, for they will see God. Life can be difficult, and it is easy to grow bitter, vindictive, angry or store toxins within. The longing for justice can make us unjust. It is in the realm and sacred place of the heart that we often need to turn to be pure. The Greek word for purity of heart means cleansing, catharsis. If we do not allow God, again and again, to burn the dross from the gold in our heart, then our passion for justice and mercy can be undermined and subverted. Jesus welcomes us to enter the castle of the soul and clean up what must be cleaned, but we are not allowed to stay there. The drawbridge must be lowered, and we will be nudged to cross the moat and enter the world again. We are not all allowed to hide away in some pietistic ghetto or assume there will be a quick and speedy resolution to the difficult dilemmas of life. Escapism and triumphalism are foreign to the Beatitudes.

What is a peacemaker?

Blessed are the peacemakers. A peacemaker is one who goes into the midst of the fray and attempts to broker reconciliation. Martin Luther King Jr. once said, 'Peace is not the absence of tension; it is the presence of justice.' Therefore, we cannot separate justice and peacemaking. Peacemaking is an active and conscious decision to be an agent of justice and reconciliation. It is not a retreating from or repressing conflict for the sake of a shallow unity. A peacemaker is a bridge-builder between two warring tribes, and often the peacemaker is shot at by both clans and their chieftains. Such though is the vocation of a just peacemaker.

Jesus concludes the Beatitudes by insisting that those who seek justice will be treated as the prophets of old. The Beatitudes are, in a most significant sense, a distillation of the Jewish prophetic vision. Such a vision knits together an in-depth journey into the mansions of the soul and a call to walk onto the stage of life to be makers of peace and agents of justice. It is this prophetic vision that is at the ethical core and center of the Christian faith. When we ignore, domesticate, sanitize or censure the script of this Magna Carta of faith, the text of our inner and outer life will lack the fullness and richness of a mature faith.

Just as it is natural for a bird to spread wide wings and take to the blue canopy, and just as it is natural for an apple tree to produce apples, so, in our new life in Christ, we cannot but live forth the Beatitudes. Our very being will be transformed into this new life, this deeper conversion, and this more profound rebirth is a delicate blend of God's inviting grace and our receptivity to such overtures of love. In Christ, our new nature is finally known, and in the Beatitudes, the scent and aroma of such a nature can be detected and picked up by the senses of the soul

When Jesus finished the Beatitudes and Sermon on the Mount, the disciples had to descend from the mountain, in a centered and more deeply informed way, to live forth the new life, and share such a transformed life with others. The good news is about being freed from the many demons (and ego within) just as it is about freeing the oppressed from the bonds of injustices. When such good news is embodied in thought, word and deed, the prophetic vision of the Beatitudes will take root and bear an abundant harvest in time.

Epilogue

The Blanket
Descends Again

By Brad Jersak

During a trip to Wales, UK, I shared many of the thoughts in this book with a precious church in Llanelli. Specifically, I was able to testify to how I see them already living their faith with Jesus' eyes, an open table, and a narrow path. Their passion for worship and justice deeply impacted my heart.

After the final session, one of their members approached me with this message:

> As I listened to you talk about the way Christ has opened up his temple and his table, I felt concerned. I found your radically open invitation troubling. I started objecting, "But Lord, *you* said this and that in your Word!"

At that point, Peter's vision in Acts 10 came to mind. I remembered how Peter saw a great sheet descending from heaven, full of unclean things. When the Lord told him, "Take and eat," Peter was shocked! He objected, "No Lord! I've never eaten anything unclean!" He *knew* what the Law—*God's Law*—said about such things. He was confident that he knew God's final word on the matter. [Does this sound familiar?] And God rebuked Peter: "Do not call anything impure that God has declared clean." Just then, some "unclean" Gentiles knocked at his door. Peter got the message.

I felt that God was telling me, "I am doing a new thing as in the days of Peter, the blanket, and my open door to the Gentiles. It is not as though I did not give this Word in the first place, but this is a new season.

"The blanket is coming down again. And you will be as shocked as Peter because you *are* godly and you *do* know my Word. Now *you* are saying, 'But Lord, *you* said...' But I am the Lord and while *I* do not change, I reserve the right to change you—to change your heart and your eyes—to change how you see my plans for this season. "

Frankly, the message alarmed me. I have no desire to teach things that contradict Scripture or sound theology. Yet I felt its weight. I realized that Peter's hesitancy to embrace the vision was rooted in a rigid forgetfulness. Had not Jesus already declared "all foods clean" (Mark 7:19)? And hadn't he repeatedly welcomed Gentiles, women, and children to his table? Hadn't the Spirit already been poured out on "all flesh" on the Day of Pentecost? Had they all forgotten so quickly? Or couldn't they see the connection? And now, how about us?

God's reminder to Peter ignited a paradigm-shattering revolution in the church. It resulted in the inclusion of Jew and Greek, male and female, slave and free (Gal. 3:28). As Peter's eyes were opened, the church remembered and responded. They began to see Christ in unexpected places and in surprising people. That is the spirit in which I hope you will weigh the thesis of this book: *remember to see.*

I leave you with a meditative exercise that may just activate your eyes to see Jesus in those you encounter today—especially in those who live on the "social edge." Now is our opportunity to be "the word made flesh"... to be Jesus to the least of these.

Meditation for Action:
Becoming the Word-made-flesh

1. Ask God to remind you of someone who might be "the least" by worldly standards. Ask God to help you see Jesus in this person. What does Christ-in-this-person need? Ask for eyes to see beneath the surface.

2. How could Christ-in-you love this person? Offer Christ your eyes, ears, mouth, hands, and feet. Ask him to give you his heart for this person. How would he have you be Jesus to him or her? Here, meditation becomes action.

3. When you reach out to this person, how did Christ reveal himself to you through him or her? Did he touch or change your heart in the encounter? Did he love you through the person? What did you experience? Why not tell them?

Appendix

Community Exercise: Open Our Eyes, Lord

Open Our Eyes, Lord [1]

Reader 1:

Open our eyes, Lord.

Community:

Open our eyes. We want to see Jesus.

Reader 1:

Behold, I will be with you always until the end of time.

Reader 2:

I see Christ in the eyes of a friend.
I see Christ in the tender touch of wrinkled hands.
I see Christ in the arms of a mother cradling a child.

---

[1] By Francine Inslee in Year A Worship Resources, ed. Jane M. Gardner, © 2004 Herald Publishing House, page 236. Used by permission from the Community of Christ.

Community:

Open our ears, Lord. We want to hear Jesus.

Reader 1:

Behold, I will be with you always until the end of time.

Reader 2:

I hear Christ in the cry of the hungry.
I hear Christ in the songs of the oppressed.
I hear Christ in the praises of the grateful.

Community:

Open our hands, Lord. We want to help Jesus.

Reader 1:

Behold, I will be with you always until the end of time.

Reader 2:

I see Christ serving soup on the streets.
I see Christ teaching people self-care.
I see Christ nursing the sick and disabled.

Community:

Open our mouths, Lord. We will witness of you:
We see Christ in the eyes of our neighbors.
We hear Christ in the sounds of pain and joy.
We see Christ in action in the world.
Lord, you are risen indeed. We are your witnesses.
You are at work in the world today.
You still call disciples to assist in the work.
We will be your disciples.
We are the disciples of Jesus Christ.

Reader 1:

Behold, I will be with you always until the end of time.

Hymn of Consecration:
Take My Life and Let It Be

Frances R. Havergal, February 1874.

*Take my life, and let it be
consecrated, Lord, to Thee.
Take my moments and my days;
let them flow in ceaseless praise.
Take my hands, and let them move
at the impulse of Thy love.
Take my feet, and let them be
swift and beautiful for Thee.*

*Take my voice, and let me sing
always, only, for my King.
Take my lips, and let them be
filled with messages from Thee.
Take my silver and my gold;
not a mite would I withhold.
Take my intellect, and use
every power as Thou shalt choose.*

*Take my will, and make it Thine;
it shall be no longer mine.
Take my heart, it is Thine own;
it shall be Thy royal throne.
Take my love, my Lord, I pour
at Thy feet its treasure store.
Take myself, and I will be
ever, only, all for Thee.*

ACKNOWLEDGEMENTS

As God works on my heart, saying thanks becomes more difficult, because it I don't really know where to start or end. My apologies to those I've missed or only mentioned by category.

Thanks to my *family* (Eden and the boys) and my church (*Fresh Wind*) for giving me time to write and for patiently loving me.

Special thanks to the *four pillars* that gathered to teach me about the Kingdom. Thanks to the many *intercessors* (the secret seven, the prayer chain, the posse, the House of Prayer, and remote intercessors from Alaska to Winkler to Wales)... I'm well covered!

Thanks to those who introduced me to the treasure in those with disabilities: John Ditchfield, Sue West, Chad Teigen. To Chris Janzen, Sava, Andy, and Circle of Friends, thanks for inviting me to your table. Thanks to all the staff at Bethesda and MCC (esp. my homegroup at Grant West) for bringing your individuals into my life and church.

Thanks to my mentors (Ron Dart, Brian West, Eric McCooeye), my co-leaders (the Peggs, MacPhersons, and the Dycks), my EA friends (esp. Mike Stewart and Eric Janzen), and Agora for weighing everything and spotting for me when I take to the limb.

Thanks to the many contributors (cf. the facing page) for taking time to tell your stories firsthand. Also, thanks to the many heroes whose stories were included in the chapters that I wrote. I'm grateful to you for giving me permission to share your lives publicly.

Thanks to the churches that take care of me while on the road. We feel a special kinship to sister churches like the Gathering, the Canopy, Seeds, WCV, Appleseed Lodge, New Life, Landsberg Vineyard, Antioch North and South... as well as God's family in Burma, Thailand, and China.

And thanks to those who helped produce the book: Kevin Miller, my band of proofreaders, designers (the Borcks), Matt Baker (for pointing me to Eugene), and the Friesens team. Finally, thanks to Eugene Peterson for the generous foreword—it felt like the Father's blessing.

CONTRIBUTORS

Eugene Peterson is Professor Emeritus of Spiritual Theology for Regent College in Vancouver, B.C. He is also known for providing us with *The Message Bible.*

Andy MacPherson is a pastor at Fresh Wind and works with people at disabilities at Bethesda Christian Association and Circle of Friends.

Ray Loewen is the founder and director of Build a Village, a ministry that works with the Mennonite Central Committee in Central America and the Middle East. He also sells cars in Altona, MB, Canada.

Dr. Marshall Rosenberg is the founder and educational director of the Center for Nonviolent Communication. He travels throughout the world mediating conflict and promoting peace.

Henri Nouwen was a Dutch priest and the pastor of the L'Arche Daybreak Community in Toronto.

Irene Jersak lives in Killarney, MB, Canada with her husband, Lloyd, where they raised Bradley and Rodney.

Jenni Kornell works with the Viva Network where she coordinates efforts to rescue child prostitutes from the sex trade and to place them in homes where they can receive healing.

Ella Rempel is a senior grandmother and intercessor to Eden Jersak.

Darla Faulkner worked with an NGO in Africa, serving as director in a home for children affected by HIV/AIDS.

Brita Miko worked at Union Gospel Mission and on the streets of Vancouver's East Side helping addicts and prostitutes.

Dr. Eric Kuelker is a registered clinical psychologist. He and his wife Heather attend Fresh Wind with their three children.

Ron Dart teaches political science and religious studies at the UCFV in Abbotsford, BC. He is also a prolific poet and writer in the area of spirituality, justice and politics.

Also available by Brad Jersak

CAN YOU HEAR ME?
Tuning in to the God who speaks
Published by Lion Hudson

A combination of biblical and historical research, real life experiences, and inspiring exercises on "listening prayer" to transform our prayers into intimate conversations—real meetings with a living Friend.

CHILDREN, CAN YOU HEAR ME?

God loves children and longs to meet with them through prayer. In every daily scenario, He reveals Himself freely to kids, speaking to them as a very best Friend.

RIVERS FROM EDEN - 40 Days of Intimate Conversation with God

A forty-day spiritual exercise designed to make "listening prayer" a life-style. It models an approach to prayer in which one's time with God becomes an intimate, interactive meeting.

FEAR NO EVIL - Breaking Free from the Culture Of Fear

Fear No Evil confronts the culture of fear beginning with snapshots of pop-angst. It then deconstructs the lies that drive fear and offers steps to healing— a spiritual journey into freedom.